How to Get to Wonderful

Ronna Helene

How to Get to Wonderful

Ronna Helene

How to Get to Wonderful
By Ronna Helene

Copyright © 2023 by Ronna Helene Webb

For more information, please see *About the Author* at the close of this book.

Cover photo by Quang Nguyen Vinh/Pexels.
Cover design and interior design and formatting by Donna Marie Benjamin.

Quotations in this book which are attributed to other authors are used by permission.

All rights reserved. No part of this publication may be reproduced, distributed, or transmitted in any form or by any means, including photocopying, recording, or other electronic or mechanical methods, without the prior written permission of the publisher, except in the case of brief quotations embodied in critical reviews and certain other noncommercial uses permitted by copyright law. For permission requests, write to the publisher, addressed "Attention: Permission Coordinator," at the address below:
Elevation Press
P.O. Box 603
Cedaredge, CO 81413

Ordering information: Quantity sales. Special discounts are available on quantity purchases by book clubs, corporations, associations, and others. For details, contact the publisher at the address above.

ISBN 978-0-932624-17-8

1. Main category— [Spiritual] 2. Other categories— [Meditation] — [Healing]

© 2023
Elevation Press
Cedaredge, Colorado
www.elevation-press-books.com

Foreword

I met Ronna Webb in the spring of 2018. I had just moved from Denver to the Colorado Western Slope to begin a new job as grief counselor for the rural hospice there. I was curious about the benefits of the energy balancing treatments that Ronna offered to staff and volunteers because I had been minimally exposed to energy work in my own grieving process after the death of my husband. Ronna made a lot of sense that day and we then became better acquainted through her times with patients. I soon invited her to become a bereavement volunteer to work with grieving families.

Ronna assisted in personal sessions with clients, and she also co-facilitated the ongoing grief group with me. In that group, Ronna opened to her own grief due to the death of her mother. Ronna was a young child when she lost her mother and her family was relatively closed when it came to expressing emotions. She, thus, wasn't encouraged to express her devastation and she held this heavy in her heart for much of her life. But while volunteering for the hospice program, Ronna finally found her own voice in her grieving process, and hence she continued the path of healing from her loss.

Our friendship grew and I've gotten to know her well. Ronna seems ageless to me. While we have a 30-year age difference between us, she seems to have more energy, more spark for life, and more youthfulness than I do. Her sense of adventure has led us down many new roads with spectacular views. She brings out the best in me in that way, where alone I may walk one mile but with Ronna I walk three.

Because of her life experiences, Ronna knows that life has its dark and its light sides. She has used the dark in her own life to heal for the better, but she never diminishes another's emotional place; she allows people to emote and discover their own feelings. Because she walks alongside, not in front of, whomever she's helping, this allows the door to open for individual healing to occur.

When I'm having a bad day, Ronna won't tell me "but you should be grateful for everything all the time." I call such an unrealistic attitude "toxic positive." Ronna will listen with care and authenticity and may say, "I will send healing thoughts your way" so then I can honor and shift my own perceptions as I see fit. When Ronna does send healing thoughts or offers a loving hand, I always find my mood improve and my perspective shift.

Our professional relationship grew as well. I was facilitating a post-polio support group for people who survived polio as children but who experience residual effects of the disease later on in life. I will always remember the first Loving Shift workshop Ronna led with this group that was open to polio survivors and their caregivers. There was one couple in which the wife was the post-polio survivor and her quiet husband had Parkinson's disease. At the end of the workshop, Ronna instructed everyone to draw how they were feeling. When we shared our drawings, this gentleman, despite his shaky hands, limited motor skills, and difficulty speaking, held up a picture of a smiling face and said, "I feel happy." That was a huge reminder of the kind of work that Ronna does: offering authentic, supportive, and caring work that opens the heart and soul and allows for healing to occur.

Over time, despite both of us relocating to different places, Ronna and I have continued to be close friends, and when she decided to write this book, I became one of her many champions. Her words are lyrical, her writing is accessible, and her stories are remarkable. You will find a little bit of you in every page due to how she speaks through the written word. I hope you enjoy Ronna's work and I hope you find peace and healing in your own life-journey.

Melanie McClanahan, MSW/MSOL
Denver, CO
01/19/2022

*This book of universal love stories is dedicated to
Erin Hilleary,
who encouraged me from the very beginning and to
Hillery McCalister
who supported me to the finish line.
I love you both.*

Characters and Terms

Mom or Mommy: my mother, Dorothy

Mama: Human way of representing divine feminine energy of unconditional love that flows through Ronna from Spirit for storytelling and healing.

Aleae: Human way of representing spiritual aspect of Ronna as divine, dancing goddess.

Birna: Human way of representing spiritual union of Spirit and Earth. Ronna acting as translator to ground divine energy on Earth.

Master and Amanda: Heroes of personal myths I wrote from my subconscious over a period of years. Master is a teacher and seeker and Amanda is the wise higher self.

Meditation Prose: Mama's stories of divine love reminding us who we are.

Visions: Inspiration, concepts and stories that come in a flash and unfold without Ronna mentally guiding them.

Personal Anecdotes: Chronicles of Ronna's triumph over human fear, involving divine love and light.

Reconnect and hear your soul talk to you.

Introduction

How to Get to Wonderful is a composite of original stories, including the loving shifts that I've personally experienced. It's my pleasure to share the awesomeness of connecting with the Universe and feeling the healing results of such all-powerful Love in my life.

I won't ask you to believe anything. I am simply sharing the magnificent energy I have felt and visions that I myself have had. I only ask of you, dear reader, to take away that which you find comforting and empowering and let it fill you up on your life's journey.

It has been a huge part of my personal healing to create this book. An acquaintance I ran into casually asked, without expecting a response, "How are you Ronna?" and I cheerfully answered, "I'm wonderful!" I can still hear Charlie's voice as his response summed up my life's work: **"How do you get to Wonderful?"**

Thanks for asking, Charlie. Here it is.

I've been to Wonderful. Wonderful is when I know fully in my heart that I am spiritually Home, aware of the love my soul carries throughout all time and space. Home is where I feel wise and secure and infinitely expansive. Home is where I know that I'm loved without question and where I love unconditionally without judgment. There is no end to this love; it just is.

"The Game of Forget" and the following loving messages from Spirit pretty much tell the thread of my healing story. I keep this first short quote posted on my desk as my personal manifesto:

**To REMEMBER and TO BE,
despite the odds,
is your greatest purpose.**

Show how it feels to be love and light
in your humanness!

To relate your journey of life and healing,
for your own catharsis, and as an inspiration for others,
is your work for this life.

Give the people some relief from the confusing times.
Let them sit back and hear stories.
Stories that are easy to absorb.
Stories that move energy.
Stories that speak to the heart.

Writing has always been of utmost importance to my well-being, even as a kid. I simply loved putting my feelings down on paper and watching the words flow into meaning. Mrs. Golding, my fourth-grade teacher, often asked me to put my poems up on the board for the other kids to read. Mr. Basow, bless his caring heart, brought me writers' magazines in the fifth and sixth grades.

My high school English teacher also encouraged me to get my poems and stories published. I had been having trouble figuring out what to write for a short story assignment for his writing class, not quite getting the concept of "Write what you know about," because I thought my own life was way too uninteresting. Under the pressure of a due date, I finally wrote a story about an unhappy youngster who had lost her mother and didn't get along with her stepmother. That's the piece my teacher wanted me to publish. I indeed wrote that story from my own experience but I was sure surprised to find out that it had universal appeal!

My writing for the next ten years or so was centered on papers for school or work, taking on the more disciplined mental aspect that was expected. I achieved academic praise but the thoughts of my heart lay buried. Eventually, my unspoken personal stories began to demand my attention. I may have appeared rather well-adjusted on the outside but I was inwardly begging for help because I so wanted to be heard.

I slowly slipped into the throes of despondency in my early forties, and though it's quite obvious in hindsight, I was surprised to be diagnosed as clinically depressed. It was a relief to know I had a condition with a name; I figured I was terribly inept or maybe crazy because no matter what I tried, I couldn't climb out of the dark hole I kept falling into. With proper medication, the world began to look a whole lot brighter and I began to breathe freely once again.

A friend had been asking for months if I would join her in one of Rosa Mazone's classes. Rosa was an incredibly successful coach who exuded a comforting aura of love and peacefulness. She is still one of my dearest idols. I had continually refused to join Rosa's presentations, though, because in my depressed state of perception I felt that it would be useless. Imagine my friend's surprise when, after about 3 weeks on medication, I signed up with her to attend one of Rosa's seminars!

Rosa worked with clients to help us see new and positive ways of looking at life, much of which was through connection with our spirit, visualization, family dynamics, intuition, and just plain-old unconditional love. I vividly remember the third gathering in this particular seminar series: Rosa wound up the evening by asking each of us to explain why we were here now in this class. When my turn came, I said only, **"I want to know who I am!"** as the tears quickly tumbled.

That was the beginning of my life-long relationship with Spirit. I would often be up talking to Spirit and filling pages in my notebooks at 2:00 or 3:00 in the morning. The format of these conversations is always the same, even to this day. I start out describing what is emotionally bothering me or what I want to understand, and soon the dialogue takes on a life of its own. Eventually, as I grasp what I need, the solution that unfolds is always Love. Always.

I was in awe when I read Neale Donald Walsch's first book, *Conversations with God*, in 1995. Hundreds of entries in my notebooks paraphrased what he wrote and some could have been direct quotes! I had no doubt whatsoever that I was connecting with divine presence; hearing the same loving message and feeling the same loving energy, available to us all.

I can still feel the amazing energy of Love swelling in me as I heard in my head, "**Speak to the beings with Love. They will listen to you because you come from real Love. And it will FILL…YOU…UP…**"

I continued to write, and read, and write. I agree wholeheartedly with an article in *The Elephant Journal* online magazine that writing, for me, is a necessity, a way to uncover stories and the power of our voice to impact the world.

I have been told by various people in the healing arts that this life is the life for me to awaken to my soul, to my own story. Now is the time for me to remember that I am a divine spark of light, no matter how challenging the current difficulties. But I must admit that there are moments when my own words sound hollow to me and I feel the heaviness of dark thoughts weighing me down.

Following such times of doubt, I always receive in some way the loving reminder to awaken to who I really am! I am reminded to open my heart and literally feel Love's warm vibration flowing throughout my being.

The powerful love-filled images in this book speak directly to the heart. Each story, allegory, or real-life anecdote exemplifies ways that I directly experienced divine universal energy in my life. The written words are here to communicate ideas, of course, but their major significance is to convey feelings of wonder. My goal in sharing such images is that they help you to experience the incredible flow of love in your own way.

These images all arose from the magic of an open connection with Spirit. Some visions came to me when gently guided in a deeply relaxed state of being, such as QHHT (Quantum Healing Hypnosis Technique) or with other professional healing guides. The myths poured from my subconscious when I sat down with an intent to record whatever came up but with no agenda beforehand. I could feel the myths almost pushing out, wanting to be born. The Mama stories of who-we-are start out as quick images and short thoughts in my mind's eye and take full form when I sit down with pen in hand to birth the concepts.

The tales I share about situations in my here-and-now life are straight from my emotional memory as if I were living it once more in that moment. By relaxing my mind and allowing memories to surface without censure, I was there again. Some details were surely forgotten or confused over time, but I assure you that my emotions and the healing love are authentically conveyed.

So many wonderful teachers have touched my life, some of them visibly for periods of time and some of them angelic; I can't say for sure that there's any difference. Their guidance was "paid forward" and now I hope to pass on how awesome it is to connect with the universal energy of Love. These visions and images are meant to stir feelings and guide you to access your own transformative wisdom in your own special way. I offer this book of Love's stories in the hope that they will fill you up and help you find your own wonderful way Home. Enjoy!

You are loved beyond measure.

Finding Mama

Mama, the spiritual archetype of divine feminine energy, has been the pillar of my life since I became aware of this energetic presence in the late 1980's when *Mama* came to me in an early morning Thanksgiving meditation in Colorado. I had prepared the turkey, put it in a low-heat oven, and went back to bed to meditate. I lost all sense of time but suddenly sat up and declared "I am *Mama*! I don't know what that means, but I'm *Mama*!"

I put on my robe, went downstairs to stoke our wood-burning stove and sat down at my computer. I spent the rest of the day writing "The Game of Forget." It was a new and fascinating experience for me as I became aware of concepts in my mind and then let the words put forth from my heart. My husband and our young daughter, bless their hearts, prepared the rest of our Thanksgiving meal as I remained absorbed in writing the story.

I've been honored with several *Mama* stories of how grand we are and how love is all there is. I hope these stories and anecdotes serve to touch the divine spark of love that resides within all of us.

"The Game of Forget" is the concept behind every message and story that I offer, sparking loving energy shifts in people's lives. With universal energy flowing within our being, we can't help but remember that we are sparks of divine love. As we joyously share this profound energy with others, love spreads wherever we go.

Meet Mama

Snuggled in her embrace
I know that I am loved beyond measure.
Love moves into every part of my being
And I know that I, too, am this love.

This is how it feels when divine energy radiates and swirls within us. The love of *Mama*, the feminine archetype of unconditional love, hugs us and holds us and allows us to relax into her sacred presence. Our beings sink into a deep sense of inner peace as our hearts join the loving energy flow with *Mama*.

This energy leads us to feel—to be there—to know— to experience for ourselves—how love heals.

It is that simple.
It is that profound.

The Game of Forget

Come my children. Gather 'round.

Sit by the warm fire. Cuddle up in your blanket.

Mama has a story for you.

This is a story about who you are. And why you're here.

And about how much I love you.

Once upon a time, a long time ago, there was a presence whom we call God.

God was always there.

He wasn't born and he didn't die.

He just *was*.

And He still is.

We often call God *He* but God isn't a man or a woman. So we will call God *He* sometimes and we will call God *She* sometimes.

God is pure Love.
Nothing less.
And there isn't anything more than pure Love.

God was everything before there was anything else in the world to be.

God, The Creator, The Love, The Light, The Divine, are all words for the same thing. Pure Love.

But because God was the whole and total universe, there wasn't anything else to think about or feel.

Thought without feelings doesn't go anywhere.
It doesn't do anything.
Thought just is.

God decided that She wanted to be more than just thought.

God wanted something to think about. God wanted something to love.
God wanted a way to show Her love. God wanted to experience Her own love. God wanted feelings.

So God thought about Herself.

As She did so,
She became very active and She began to
E X P A N D.

The Love kept getting greater and greater,
until the Love burst forth into a zillion new sparks of light!

Now, instead of being God all by Herself,
God became sparks of god-love and god-light
all over the place!

One day a bunch of god-lights were chatting when they came up with a big idea. "Okay," they said, "Let's take our pure energy of love and create a world we can actually see. All we have to do is think about what we want and we'll have it. This will be fun!"

The god-lights thought mountains
   and rivers
      and clouds
         and flowers
           and animals
             into being.

Their thoughts really worked!
Now there was god-love everywhere, in every form!

Remember, children, since the god-lights created the world from their own thoughts, everything was really still God.

Soon the god-lights wanted to
>   smell the flowers,
>>   feel the wind,
>>> and pet the animals that they had formed.

So the next thing they did was create bodies in order to get about on this earth. They were still the pure light, of course, but having bodies was like putting a coat over their light-selves so that they could be seen.

The god-lights would come and go from their earth playground as they wished because all they had to do was think themselves back into their lighter form.

>   Life became really interesting.

Each being had the opportunity to create and experience whatever it wanted. All of God's newly created sparks of light could now go out and have adventures.

They could actually share love and touch the creations that came from their love.

After a long time and lots of experimenting, things settled down a bit. This physical world became pretty comfortable and life was a whole lot of fun! The god-beings would stay for longer and longer periods of time before going back to check in with the lighter world.

So for fun, the god-lights decided that they needed to add some challenge to their times on the earth.

So they invented a game called **_FORGET_**.

The main idea of the game was to forget why they were here and see how long it took to remember.

The earth god-lights would pretend to forget that the whole reason they were here was to experience their love on the earth. They would not remember that they were here to have feelings about the things they created from their pure thought.

It seemed to be a safe enough game because they still knew that they were the light and nothing could happen to them. They knew where Home was and that they could be in contact with all the other god-lights any time they wanted.

All they had to do was think about it.

These earth god-lights were very adventurous. They really got into the *Game of Forget*. The rules of the game kept growing and changing and they added new challenges all the time.

Bit by bit, the forgetting got greater.

The beings began to forget that they were all exactly the same god-light and they started to believe that some beings were better than others. They even began to believe that they were only their physical selves.

THEY FORGOT WHERE HOME WAS.

THEY FORGOT WHO THEY REALLY WERE.

So fear soon developed and the beings in this world felt afraid. They thought they were lost and alone in the world they created.

THE GAME OF FORGET WAS NO LONGER A GAME.

We, as god-beings on the earth, are still playing the game. We come in from the lighter world knowing who we really are but we get caught in the powerful *Game of Forget*.

If you stop for a minute, you may remember. Somewhere within you, a feeling might be stirring.

I am telling you this, dear children, so that you can remember who you really are. And why you are here.

We have played the game long enough; we are here now to remember. It is time to look at where we have been and make our choices about where we want to go.

You can do this. Each of you.

You are god-light.

We are all one.
We are all exactly the same Love.

We are here to find ourselves.
We are here to bring Light to Earth.
We are here to be Love again.

You are divine light. Share the light with whomever you touch.

Love in the OR

December 2000

It was one of those typical family sad-news notifications that heralded a huge shift in my life. I was living in Germany at the time my older brother emailed me that our younger sister had just been diagnosed with breast cancer.

My thoughts began swirling: "Oh my God, what shocking news! What do I say to her?! How does anyone deal with having breast cancer?!"

I felt a bit awkward about calling her because we hadn't shared a phone call in years, so I emailed her with concern. To be honest, I really didn't know how to approach this terrible news with her person-to-person.

Well, the Universe showed me.

A couple of weeks later, I made an appointment for my annual woman's exam. I had actually forgotten that it was due because I was going to start teaching English in Frankfurt, an hour's train ride away, and my life was pretty busy. But at the last minute, I decided not to take the position so I filled one of my now-open time slots with a doctor's appointment.

I don't believe much in coincidences but I do believe that our soul, our heart, our spirit speaks clearly to us. The challenge is learning how to listen...and then how to act...and ask questions...and suddenly remember things...and cancel events...and choose doctors...

Coincidence that the Frankfurt job didn't feel like the right thing to do at the moment? What led me to making the decision to free up my time?

Coincidence that I had time now and "just remembered" that I was due my woman's annual exam? What reminded me that my exam was due?

Coincidence that the German doctor was also a radiology specialist with equipment in his office?

Coincidence that I picked this particular doctor?

Yes...indeed...he detected the lump.

Coincidence that it was almost one month to the day after I had wondered how my sister could deal with having breast cancer?

Coincidence that the surgeon I was to see was the only one available around New Year's and that his skills were highly touted above the others?

Coincidence that there was time for my biopsy within a few days, when the wait was normally several weeks?

I kept a journal of this life-changing time, both because I knew I would forget things and because I needed to verbalize and process my emotions.

Ronna's Breast Cancer Journal
January 2, 2001

Thoughts before the impending biopsy

As I see it now, I have several options:
» I can go into depression and feel hopeless about this lump in my breast.
» I can be angry and exclaim, "Why me?"
» I can be in denial.
» I can depend on others to be my strength and have none myself.

However, I choose to:
» be strong and determined,
» see myself as healthy,
» take hold of my life and shift my outlook to positive and beautiful.
» divest myself of others' opinions and decline to take their energy on for myself, as symbolized by a growing unwelcome tumor.
» have love and peacefulness in my life.
» follow my heart and heal with love.

Hear me God. Hear me loved ones. Hear me higher self. Hear me angels and guides. Hear me my soul. Be with me. Help me to heal. I ask for health and for inner strength and for a constant vision of my life as beautiful and perfect.

My life IS beautiful and perfect. It is MY life to live in beauty and peace and in service of love.

So be it.

After the biopsy, before the surgery

- » I ask for clarity about this cancer. I can't see beyond my human fear at this point. I need the understanding from my heart, not from my fear. I trust you, dear ones, to answer me clearly and without doubt this morning.
- » My absolute intent is to get these foreign bodies out of my body forever. To have room only for that which is good for me. To be loving. To truly live in grace.
- » I see clearly how I must, indeed, experience certain things in life and how I have the choice to grow from them. I am absolutely not ready to die. I intend to be healthy and to take good care of my dear body and my heart and my mind. For a very long time in this life.
- » I accept this cancer as an episode, and I ask for absolute guidance in the transformation of my life into love. Spirit, you have told me so many times that Love is All that Matters.

» I am so grateful for my most loving friends and family. And for the wonderful love that I feel right now rushing through my body.
» I keep my channels open for the answer to my question. And I keep the love flowing every second.

Thank you. I love you.

I was very frightened for my major surgery. Not only was I nervous about how much of my breast would be removed and what they would find, but I was terrified about general anesthesia as well. I also feared dying on the operating table, never waking up again.

I was also concerned about the "truth" that would come uncensored out of my subconscious. I told my family not to pay attention if I said weird things while on the drugs.

After 4 hours of surgery, they removed the lump and a fair amount of breast tissue.

The first thing I remember that morning in the recovery room is the face of the anesthesiologist. He was so angelic-looking to me; I swear I could see him glowing. I kept telling him how wonderful and kind he is.

I announced to whoever was listening that I love my family and that they love me and that I have so many loving friends. How lucky I am.

...Not bad for truth serum...

After closer examination by the lab a bit later, the margins were not clear of cancerous cells and so they must excise more in a week or so. The doctor suggested also removing my lymph nodes to avoid any cells squeaking past the margins.

A harrowing 10 days later

Today is the day before I go into the surgery. I am still in a quandary about removing my lymph nodes. Do I have the surgeons take only one or two sentinel nodes and wait a week to hear lab results? Or do I live with the fear that they missed some cells and I need yet another operation? Or do I let them take basically all of the lymph nodes in the hopes that the cancer cells will be removed and there is no place for new ones to travel? Will I face a lifetime of possibilities of swelling, numbness, fear of infection, lessened mobility, etc.?

God I am tired.....I am going through the motions of living each day but I can't help looking through this murky haze of anxiety.

Dr. Tieva had planned for general anesthesia again for this second major surgery, but we quickly got him to agree that local anesthesia would be fine and would cause much less stress to my already-overstressed mind and body. Both physicians agreed that they would forego the tube down my throat. I would be awake and could talk but I would remember nothing.

I was relatively calm that morning until we arrived at 6:00 and the hospital technician told me that my surgery wasn't scheduled until 11:00. They had told me yesterday that the surgery was to be done at 7:30 am because Dr. Tieva had cancelled some other procedures in order to have me be the first one on the schedule.

Well, I finally flipped! I let my anger rip for the first time in this ordeal! I told the technician in no uncertain terms that it was unfair to make me wait and they had no business giving me false information! They need to get it together! I have reached my limit!!

Then I cried and cried and cried.

Major Lohse, a special nurse whom I liked from the first operation, put my husband, Peter, and me in a room alone so that I could calm down or rave or do whatever I needed. She hurriedly went to the operating area to get Dr. Tieva.

Dr. T came in within five minutes, along with some administrator who apologized because it was her night clerk who had not entered the proper time in the log. Dr. Tieva agreed that this was too much already and told me that indeed I was scheduled for the first surgery.

Then he shortened his surgeon's distance and gave me a loving and comforting hug. His kind treatment helped me to shift my emotions somewhat and I quit spinning out of control. By now it was 7:30 am and time to get the procedure over with.

As we walked into the surgery area, Tamara (the surgical nurse who remembered me from the previous procedures) came bouncing up and gave me a huge smile and a great big hug! I said jokingly that we had to quit meeting like this. A new anesthesiologist came in and looked at me a bit quizzically, asking if we had met before, but we agreed that we had not, at least not in this life.

I remember him asking me the usual questions about allergies and meals but all else is tucked away in a drug-induced amnesia until I woke up on the operating table.

We were still in the operating room because they were waiting for the pathology report on the tissue they removed today. The anesthesiologist, Tamara and Dr. T were all chatting and I really felt like I was with old friends. The anesthesiologist asked me if I was a very religious person. I replied, "No. I'm highly spiritual but not religious. Why do you ask?" They both told me that I was mumbling throughout the procedure **"This is an operation of Love."**

As they said that, I was washed with the awareness of being totally surrounded by guides, loved ones, healers and white light. I could sense that the room was packed to capacity with light beings. I felt totally taken care of with the greatest love and compassion and I grasped that this whole breast cancer experience is part of a higher purpose. I had no doubt whatsoever that I am constantly surrounded with love.

Once the pathologist called back and told Dr. T that the tissue samples were clear, they told me that I could go straight back downstairs because I was doing surprisingly well. As they wheeled me back on the gurney, we were still chatting and smiling and I heartily wished another patient good morning. Peter said that he was at first a bit frightened at my behavior, wondering what kind of drugs they had given me.

Obviously I was full of the most powerful "mood-lifter" in creation. Ain't Love grand?!

Back in the same-day-surgery room in my little curtain-enclosed cubicle, we all talked a bit and I was still cheery and animated. Major Lohse had herself bought me a sandwich and I scarfed it like I hadn't eaten all day! (Of course I hadn't.) We all joked with the technician who kept taking my blood pressure, and even got him to giggling. Before long he told me that I could get dressed and go home.

The Chaplain

As we were waiting for my official discharge, I heard the Army chaplain come into the room. My gut reaction was "Oh brother, I don't need preaching..." but I instantly shifted my opinion and decided that it would be just fine to welcome him. He struck me as a small and rather insecure man. As he walked past the curtains, he first looked at my daughter in confusion and then realized she wasn't the patient. Then he looked at me with such pity in his eyes, I felt sorry for him!

He immediately started going on about how much I have endured. Said something akin to "You poor woman. You've been through so much. It's terrible. I remember when my wife got that 'Big C' call from her mother."

I couldn't imagine how his carrying on with such pitiful remarks was supposed to be comforting or supportive, but I refrained from rolling my eyes. He was at least trying to help.

I simply looked calmly into his eyes and said in a most luxurious, slow, encompassing voice, "As you know in your business, every experience is a challenge to look at the positive and learn from it." I didn't feel preachy or know-it-all; the loving words flowed naturally from deep within my being.

I wish that I had had a camera to capture his expression, but I will never forget this moment.

The chaplain's eyes opened wide in a look of total shock and his jaw literally dropped open. He stood speechless.

Then suddenly, as if he were pushed from behind, he was down on one knee in front of me, fingers entwined and head down in a prayer position. The moment was frozen in time before he muttered to himself and skittered away.

During the physical operation, my conscious mind was quiet and my being was embraced by Spirit. Upon returning to conscious awareness, I was still flooded with light and profound love; that is what everyone in the room got to experience. Still deeply connected with Spirit, the peacefulness filled the space and beyond.

And the love continues to spread.

Yes, this was indeed an Operation of Love.

The Womb of Love

Come my children, *Mama* is here.

Expand with your awareness of me, divine Love.
    Melt into me.
        Feel us as One.

Remember floating in the womb of divine Love:
    calm
        safe
            secure
                sacred

Feel the Love expand within you and beyond.
    Love fills every space.
        Love is All There Is.

Now reach out to Mother Earth and imagine a magnificent tree that has been growing for generations.
    Breathe in its earthy smell and taste the heavenly sap flowing from its trunk.
        Put your arms around the tree.
            Let your head rest on its trunk.
                Allow the natural love of the tree to flow into you.
    Feel the tree open up and take you into its womb.
    Feel the divine womb of Love within which you are always held.

Take a deep breath and feel Love flow within every part of your being.

Let Love flow throughout the earth, throughout the heavens,
    Far beyond where the eye can see,
        Far beyond touch and feel.

Nurture Love.

    Birth Love

        with every breath you take.

Universal Love is unlimited with no shape, no form, no solid description. It flows and vibrates in our bodies, the only place we can feel.

No Separation

I got a fascinating glimpse this morning of my true nature. In real time, the vision lasted only seconds, way faster than it will take to put my insight into words. But that's inspiration: understanding comes to mind in an all-encompassing flash and the details unfold later.

I was relaxed into a meditation when images of different parts of my life flashed simultaneously through my mind like a living kaleidoscope. I realized in that flash that these aspects make up who I am today, including both earthly experiences and divine aspects of my soul manifesting on Earth. These archetypes are **human ways of focusing and expressing the magnificence of divine energy** in this realm.

I saw little Ronna and felt again her trials and loneliness, as well as her happy childhood moments. It was crystal clear in that instant that divine guidance has held my hand and whispered in my ear throughout my life.

Ronna-now came into the vision with her years of experiences and I instantly understood how my life's choices, large or smaller, have created the details of *my* unique earth-spiritual journey. The never-ending flow of life now makes perfect sense since I deeply grasped that everything we do and everyone we see, literally *everything*, is connected in ways we can't even imagine.

As the vision quickly unfolded, my heart swelled with the familiar nurturing and wise energy of *Mama*, the spiritual storyteller who's the symbol of divine feminine energy and unconditional love. The *Mama* energy I have joyously shared for decades has touched many lives and soothed many a soul. This special energy flows through me every time I am focused on healing, speaking, writing, or just quietly being. Sharing this divine energy has been the greatest gift of my life.

After a couple of years channeling *Mama's* love-energy, I was relaxing against a tree in the Rocky Mountains and I asked in meditation to know more about my life's purpose. The bold letters "ALEAE" flashed across my mind. This spiritual identity resonated deeply within me and I felt its strength long before I discovered its significance. *Aleae* is for me an energy symbol, or archetype, of the divine goddess who dances and sings and simply creates joy wherever she goes. She, like *Mama*, exudes unconditional love that reminds us of Home. When I am carefree and light, I often envision myself dancing and twirling up to the stars, ensconced in *Aleae* energy.

I also saw *Birna* in my kaleidoscope vision. *Birna*, the most current of the divine aspects to be presented to me, represents the union of Universe and the personality, grounding divine energy on Earth. You will see how I have come to use this aspect of myself when you read the healing story, *"Welcome Birna."*

The Chief showed up in this fast-moving vision as well; he brought a welcome balance to my feminine aspects. I earlier had seen myself as the *Chief* in a past life regression led by a Quantum Healing Hypnosis Technique (QHHT) professional. At first I witnessed myself as a young warrior honored by his tribe, being prepared to lead them. Then I viewed him proudly standing in old age, having had a full life as a wise, kind leader. I can still feel the confident peace and love exuding from this beautiful being.

We tend to ascribe names to the unseen because it's easier for our minds to comprehend personalities than it is to deeply grasp boundless infinity and endless love. Each of these facets or archetypes were introduced in deep meditation to help me understand and accept these divine attributes as parts of myself, my very soul.

Mama, Aleae, Birna, the Chief, the Master, and *Amanda* are human ways of expressing divine energy. They convey choices and patterns of how I have lived, or do live, or want to live my life. In actuality, there is no separation between these personalities or energies; they are all facets of my human personality and of universal attributes and they work as a team to help create my life. I guess you could say *I am a village!*

It continues to amaze me how much knowledge is contained in the subconscious. The first *Mama* story, "*The Game of Forget,*" came to me in the late 1980s. Honest in its simplicity, its message of love remains universal and timeless.

Letting my subconscious lead the way, I wrote *The Master* stories over a period of two or three years, starting out as an exercise to unfold my personal myth. As these myths kept coming to me, it became clear that the *Master*, though set in ancient times, was unfolding my current personal journey of trials and healing.

The *Master* is a seeker and a teacher, and he's full of questions about life. You will see how he meets up with his wise higher self, *Amanda*, and together they join with people spreading love from village to village. I am ever grateful to be sharing that love now.

I'm still in the process of internalizing this concept of our multi-faceted selves. I've been writing for decades about the divine light within each of us but it's the blissful ***experience*** of ***feeling*** our expansive energy that enables me to truly grasp that we *are* the divine light itself.

It gives me great joy to share my healing journeys. Every time I speak of universal energy and the flow of divine love, my heart expands and the bliss enfolds me. What's not to love?

Meeting *Aleae*

My awareness of the ever-flowing energy of the Universe is so exciting! Visions, like this one, where I feel the power of divine energy moving within my being create an incredibly rich and satisfying life.

My life here on this earth keeps growing with grace every time I access my higher soul's wisdom. I play, dance, walk, talk, and write to free my creativity and open space for my light to beam! I always know that I have touched Home when my heart swells with lightness as divine energy flows in every cell of my being. I do my utmost to consciously remember that I'm never alone and I am always cleverly reminded that I am the light when I inevitably forget that knowledge in my humanness.

The following *Aleae* story illustrates an oft-continuing pattern where I go from peaceful, to feeling alone again, then back to remembering who I am and how divine that is. This vision in which I meet *Aleae*, the glorious dancing goddess aspect of my soul, unfolded as I first saw young Ronna walking by herself on a sunny beach.

Ronna:
Ahhh… I love the warm white sand bunching under my feet, keeping me in direct touch with Mother Earth. My mind drifts away with the spell-binding ocean music and my heart is totally at peace now…there simply is nothing else to be, but peaceful.

Wow! I'm not alone here! Bright colorful lights are twinkling everywhere: above my head, under my feet, up to the clouds! The most magnificent sound of gentle tinkling fills the air. It's absolutely magical!! I know this brilliant light of *Aleae*, the dancing goddess aspect of my soul.

Here I go, whirling on the sand with arms flung, legs flying, my colorful skirt spinning in circles, swirling so fast I'm light as air! I'm sparkling with movement; reds, yellows, blues, greens, purples, all different hues of light are moving and intertwining like a giant kaleidoscope!

The colors swirl and curl like smoke around my body as muscles relax and my being expands! These points of light make even greater music and spin deliciously with me to create a perfect picture of joyous, dancing energy. Whee! Watch me spiraling ever upward to dance among the stars!

While expressing as *Aleae*, joyously spinning and whirling, I become simultaneously aware of young Ronna, slumped on the sand and crying out to the sky, "Oh *Aleae*, I love how it feels to be so free! But I'm afraid that now you're off to dance in the universe and you're leaving me behind as this body on the sand."

And I, as Ronna, hear *Aleae's* words in my head:

"I see you sitting there dejectedly on the sand because you think that you got left behind; but that's far from the truth. You're always connected to me, this part of your soul that dances and travels the Universe.

Really, my dear, you can't ever be left behind. You're one of the millions of divine sparks of light spreading love in the Universe. You have sparked off to experience this earth realm, but all you have to do is be still and breathe to remember that you are part of everything there is.

This is the lifetime when you wake up to the knowledge of who you are. If you were to move totally into the higher realms right now, that would mean you died. You don't want your spirit to leave your body at this time; you've asked to experience more earth life. You've agreed to keep learning how to love.

Continue feeling the high vibrations of your soul and show others how to touch their own light frequency. Such joy is a perfect way to experience your higher, lighter-than-air, expanded-self within your physical body.

Keep spinning with life and let any doubts dissolve into the light.

Dance with the stars whenever you like, but remember the beautiful task you have of spreading light on this earth."

Still feeling glorious, my vision returns to little Ronna crouched on the beach. But this time, she stands up tall and floats into the sky, leaving points of colorful light to dance on the sand. The lights await her return to the earth and will join her in spreading love from being to being.

Life is how you see it.

Bungee Jumping Perspectives

With new-found spiritual safety, I keep peeling back the emotional layers I built over years to protect myself. Lately I have been getting deep insights about the unexpressed anger I've been dragging around. I went to bed yesterday feeling the deep rage that has secretly smoldered within my being; my dark emotions were carried crushing.

The following story relates a powerful learning for me about how my perceptions do indeed create my reality. This night, I was once again triggered by unfair criticism and fell deep in the wallows of self-judgment. It felt as if my emotions were literally pinning me down; I squirmed and wrestled to get away from the uncomfortable feelings but they only tightened their grip. My mind kept jumping from one chastising thought to another, each one pulling me into a downward depressive spiral.

I wrote my thoughts down as they came stomping in, hoping to reduce the emotional chaos my despair was creating. Exhausted after an hour or so, I could finally take a deep breath and back off from my internal drama for a short moment. I became calm enough to ask the Universe that I be renewed in energy and filled again with love. As I slept, the Universe did the healing work and I woke up with renewed awareness of my divine connection.

That next afternoon, I revisited my journal entry, wincing at the despair I had recorded the night before. I picked up the notebook and naturally began to respond with a more positive way to see these situations. I countered each self-questioning in the margins of my notebook as if I were editing the notes.

The healing shift was awesome! My self-perspectives were clearly the opposite of the night before!

The Journal Entry
January 18, 4:30 a.m.

Am going through another agonizing night of being unable to fall back to sleep. My head is whirling with dark thoughts rapidly stumbling over one another. Life is crushing right now, disconnecting me from any sense of rationality or peace.

My anxious energy is all too familiar, but this strong anxiety is way more demanding of my attention than usual. Why am I doing such a number on myself? I'm sucked into the scary memories of harsh voices berating me, reiterating my fallacies and my little inner voice keeps telling me to run! Hide!

I keep ruminating on the idea that I have made up silly stories about my life, thinking I will accomplish this, teach that, have wealth, have clients, publish books...

I can't reconcile this dichotomy tonight:

On one hand, I can feel the sting of being told by people I trusted that I am weak and inept. More than once people have admonished me for showing weakness, or hurting someone's feelings, or being unaware of what I am doing. This is sometimes preceded by "You are so spiritual and speak of love, how can you......" Shame...

On the other hand, I recall countless situations in which people I trust have expressed that they see me as kind, powerful and spiritually connected. Friends, clients, even some family, thank me for helping them to see a new perspective and feeling their energy flow. Admiration...

Someone recently expressed her opinion that I don't initiate much. She thinks I wait for someone else to have ideas and then go along, painting me as a benign follower.

Events and energy healings themselves are wonderfully successful but my outreach in that realm has often fizzled. How do I deal with the games and rules of marketing that constantly change?

I feel like I've been punched in the gut... slouched over and holding my knees in despair. I'm so depleted... So powerless... Please show me the way out, loved ones...

After a long silent pause, I quit my ramblings and am aware that my energy has slightly shifted. I can feel power return to my being as I breathe more easily and relax my aching heart. Constricted shoulder and back muscles are graciously letting go of their tension. I sense myself lifting out of the depressive fog that has gripped me so tightly.

It's 5:30 a.m. and this is the voice I now hear in my head:

I can deal with change in life because I know that the true me is a constant.

The true me is my soul, my light, my grace, my power, my beauty.

My connection with Spirit is ever-expanding.

I will sleep peacefully now and wake up renewed later this morning. I will be full of energy and love and creativity. I will move forward in spreading this love.

So be it.

I awoke a few hours later feeling calm and confident. The dark feelings of the previous night were blissfully gone! That same afternoon as I stretched out for meditation, I heard inner voices again but this time they were not from my wounded ego. Spirit's voices told me kindly that worry is totally wasted energy. They reminded me that earth is a playground and I should lighten up.

After meditation, I idly picked up the notebook that lay open on my bed with last night's anguished entry. I saw the same words I wrote at 4:30 in the morning but this time I took them in from a loving and connected perspective; so I wrote comments to myself in the margins. This turned out to be a super valuable tool for healing.

Below is a repeat of some of last night's lonely, anxious perceptions, followed by thoughts from my connected and expanded outlook.

I am on a healing journey and continuously getting new self-realizations. Some of them are a challenge to bear witness to in the beginning, but they are there to be released and healed.

...I am unable to stop ruminating on the belief that I have made up wishful stories about my life, all my life.

I have indeed accomplished these very positive stories in different forms over and over again, through many years! I have diverse loving, creative experiences that fill me up every time.

The yammering voices were formed when I was belittled in the past and took such harsh messages as truth. That self-doubting energy is still stuck in parts of my being and comes up to haunt me when it gets triggered by unfair criticism. Again, it is essential that I understand, forgive, release and heal such self-doubts.

...Someone recently expressed her opinion that I don't initiate much. She thinks I wait for someone else to have an idea and then go along...

What about the many successful seminars I developed and presented in Germany and Maryland and Colorado? What about my being willing to pick up and move to a new town in my seventies? What about the contacts and friends I made in this new place? What about my growth? These are the things I care about. What part of me is she looking at?

...Events and energy healings are wonderfully successful but my outreach in that realm has too often fizzled...

Bullshit! Counting numbers of "successes" is a worthless effort. My beautiful work is far-reaching because everyone who is touched by love then spreads the love to others. The growth is exponential and cannot be quantified in any way whatsoever.

...I deal with change in everyday life because the true me is a constant. The true me is my soul, my light, my grace, my power, my beauty...

Indeed. Deeply realizing who I truly am is the way to heal my life. It is up to me to remember and live my miraculous connection to all life.

...I will sleep peacefully now and wake up renewed later this morning. I will be full of energy and love and creativity. I will move forward in spreading this love. So be it...

I am calm, I am light, I flow with divine energy. I dismiss all need to treat myself harshly in any way. I know that love is my guide and whenever I feel lost, I simply ask for clarity.

So it is.

Further Perspective
12 Days Later

Over the years I have had quite a few dreams about teaching and it is always the same situation: I would simply not show up for work or if I was supposed to substitute teach, I never got there. Never called. Didn't fill out lesson plans, didn't correct work, didn't record grades. I didn't want to teach but I thought I had to, so I constantly rebelled at my obligations.

In my awake world, I had been a conscientious teacher but after 5-6 years, I was losing interest in the routine and wanted to explore other opportunities. I became increasingly interested and involved in the metaphysical, spiritual side of life. In hindsight, it's clear to me that the coaching/teaching successes I have witnessed with all ages are due to my innate desire to help people heal and empower themselves.

In that vein, the following healing dream showed me a very important perspective: I was about to start another year of teaching and I put off the task by starting unimportant conversations with people in order to avoid the inevitable. Knowing that I could no longer stall, I dejectedly headed toward my classroom. Halfway there, I stopped in my tracks and announced that I was going to resign. Immediately.

I declared that I was no longer willing to do something that made me unhappy! No more no-shows. No more rebellion. I walked straight to the office and told them I quit! Then and there! End of dream.

I woke up feeling great relief and lusciously empowered! I could feel the new healing shift taking place. As I lay under the quilt with my cat snuggled on my chest, I let out a long, deep sigh. Joining in the release of energy, my shoulders sank deeper into the mattress as feelings and revelations floated gently through my consciousness. I was glimpsing past and present behaviors in which I was not particularly my best self. I was reminded of times of pettiness, selfishness, insecurity, and definitely times of judgment.

But this time I experienced neither remorse nor guilt nor self-chastisement. I was allowing myself to be kindly guided to these times of self-awareness so that I could perceive aspects that I hadn't recognized in myself before now. I felt as if I was being shown a mini life-review from my Loved Ones as I experienced a compassionate understanding of my behaviors, like a veil of fog had been lifted.

Just a couple of weeks ago I felt disconnected from love and was overwhelmed by feelings of sadness and guilt and self-deprecation. This morning's experience was the culmination of my commitment to change with the help of the Universe. I'm quiet, inside and out, and it feels wonderful. Peacefulness flows all around me. What a wonderful, loving way to be treated. And to treat myself as well!

Universal Love is everything *but it takes the human heart to share this energy.*

Holding Hands in the Pandemic

Standing under the hot shower in my warm little bathroom, I was casually musing on what a confusing time this Spring of 2020 is…We all are feeling lonesome and worried…We're quarantined because of COVID-19, wondering what this new sickness really is…People are missing out on their usual holiday celebrations, the restaurants are closed, the streets are empty…and now here comes the snow…

The energy surrounding me suddenly became very still and I could sense a private little bubble forming around my space. My mental focus shifted from casual meanderings to experiencing deep emotions as an inner vision washed over me.

As with the majority of my visions and spiritual messages, the understandings were instantaneous and timeless. Though the actual time elapsed in this vision couldn't have been more than a minute or two, I was experiencing people and events from the past, through the present, and into the future.

The shower disappeared from my cozy house in Colorado and my awareness was transported to the ghettos in Europe in the beginnings of WWII. I was right there, sharing the heavy despair of the people quarantined behind walls, shut off from a world in which they had been active and productive, left to walk only in their isolated enclosure. My heart was heavy as I longed to be able to rid them of their despair. Pausing to take a deep breath, my heart opened wide to energetically hug each one as they collectively cried, "What's happening? What will become of us? Why have we been imprisoned like this?"

My vision then followed these souls to concentration camps in Germany. I observed lines of men and women and children, being separated again into smaller groups. I saw the bleak buildings with bars on the entryways, the lifeless gray sky matching the fears of those being ordered about. Their fear and confusion was literally palpable and I felt my heart begin to close because it wanted to protect me from the indescribable pain.

Watching the dark scenario, my mind was whirling with questions. How could such a situation take place? How are these souls coping? What prompted such hate to grow in the minds of those who spewed total disregard for human life?

My focus shifted like a camera moving to record a new scene. I saw sick people with no chance of improvement and I clearly felt in my gut the hopelessness and pain during the pandemic of 1918, over a hundred years ago. Then in a new flash, I saw conglomerates of wars and abuse throughout our human history. Is this our legacy? What must we do to stop such heartache?

Immediately following that question, I was conscious of present times, feeling pain and isolation in multitudes around the globe. I had mental images of refugee camps, of immigration lock-downs, of long-term residents stripped of their freedom by greedy governments. In a split second I viewed religious wars, political wars, crashing economies and democracies being swept under the rug of lies and deception. All the while, human ignorance and selfishness lends a blind eye to this continuing legacy.

I instantly grasped today's viral pandemic as a metaphor for the separateness and hate that we as a whole have allowed to seep into the hidden corners of our hearts; I questioned our ability to stop the march of the debilitating virus. If history is once again repeating itself, is it even possible to seize this opportunity to make new healthy choices?

And with this question, my vision shifted yet again. Still standing in the steam of the shower, I drew my hands together and interlaced my fingers. There I was with my spiritual light beaming out, connecting with all hearts in solidarity. I felt black hands, beige hands, brown hands, all locked together, all connected to beating hearts, all connected in love.

I understood that *this* vision is our future, *if we allow it*. I heard that when we honestly open our hearts, we'll see that we are all connected and that our connection is divine. Spiritual connection has no religion, no nationality, no gender. The energy of real unconditional love leaves absolutely no room for hate or despair or loneliness.

I had more questions arise: Does it seem impossible to shift our circumstances, given our present global state of affairs? Do we want to return to the "normal" or can we globally shift to a new everyday paradigm of compassion and caring? Can we connect with one another outside of a catastrophe? Will we take the time we have now in this shutdown to begin an internal shift to love?

My high energy began to wane and my visions slowed down. This powerful magic time ended with a simple and powerful visualization:

> *Stop for just one minute every day. Breathe in deeply and feel the energy of your heart opening. Breathe out slowly and feel your loving energy moving out beyond space and time through your fingertips. Interlace your fingers and imagine that you are connecting with all other loving beings. Breathe deeply again into this connection.*

This vision will absolutely create change because we indeed change the world collectively, one person at a time, together. Let us no longer be separated.

The expansive energy stayed strongly in my awareness as I dried off and hurried to record this magical vision with which my muses graced me.

The Birth of Love

The Void

The darkness goes beyond black.
The darkness goes beyond the absence of light. Light has yet to be born.

>Quiet. Stillness.

The stillness goes beyond silence.
Silence is the absence of sounds where once there was sound. Sound has yet to be born.

Yet, here is Love,
the unlimited vibration that goes beyond measurement.

Throughout the darkness, throughout the silence,
here is absolute, profound Love.

>Love Is All There Is.

It takes limits to create a definition. Love has no definition.

Love has no description.

Love Is.

I Am

I feel the beginnings of movement.
I quiver ever so slightly with the vibration of Life.
The vibration of Life created from the unlimited vibration of Love.

I sense gentle movement.

Love Is.

I slowly tumble over in my womb of silence.

Sparks of light ignite in the womb. Light that did not earlier exist
in the unlimited vibration of Love.

I see.
I feel.
I sense an identity: I Am this Love.

I Am this Light.
I Am coming into being.

For the first time ever,
I sense vibration pushing me forward, propelling me forward.
I am bursting from the womb of Love.
I sense being born.

There was the stillness beyond silence.
There was the dark beyond light.
And there still is.

But now, there is light.
There is sound.
There is the vibration and the music
and the joy of creation!

Love, the original Light, has now birthed itself.
It's time for Love to spread.

I Am

Love lasts forever.

Mommy Dies

Mommy, do you really have to go there again?!

Mom was heading for Murphy's, a large family restaurant owned and run by my grandparents. They worked long, hard hours and my mother would often go over to help them out. It was a bit of a family affair; my brothers were often hired as busboys and my job was to test the hot fudge sundaes.

Yes, honey, Grandma needs me to hostess tonight. Come with me for a while and then Larry will take you over to spend the night at Jane's.

Okay! Tomorrow was the last day of sixth grade so Jane and I would get to stay up late! I was used to being at the restaurant for a couple of hours on school nights; my simple routine was to gather my school stuff, give my mom a goodnight hug and off I would go.

I hugged Mom as usual, stretched up on my toes to kiss her cheek, and headed for the door with my brother. But halfway there I stopped in my tracks because I felt a really strong need to hug Mommy again. I left my brother waiting for me as I ran back to throw my arms around mom's waist and hold on super tightly.

I love you Mommy!

Of course you do Ronni. I love you too. But don't be silly; go on to Jane's now. I'll see you tomorrow.

And off I went!

At 3:00 that morning, Jane's mom woke me up and gently told me to get dressed because my uncle Don was there to pick me up. I was too sleepy and too surprised to ask questions but my stomach dropped hard. Uncle Donnie?! 3:00?!

During our 5-minute drive home, Donnie told me that Mom had had a heart attack and died.

Silence. Disbelief. Confusion. Shock.

I ran into the house screaming, *Mommy! Mommy!* but my aunt met me at the door. She told me not to go into the bedroom because it would be better if I didn't see my mom that way. She held me tightly when the EMTs took my mother's body away.

And off she went.

I managed to function the rest of that summer but I did so behind the thick wall of surrealism. That fog, of course, was for my protection; otherwise how could I, an 11-year-old child, process the sudden death of my mama. For months I thought I heard her voice and would run to see my mom, only to be jerked back into the harsh reality that she was gone.

I clearly remember sitting in music class that Fall, watching different kids get called out to meet with the junior high counselor and I so wished that they would pull me out too. But, unfortunately, my good-girl-I-am-fine mask was working perfectly so no one seemed to notice my grief. I began to convince myself that losing my mother at such a young age made me stronger (ha!)

and more mature (ha!) In truth, her death left a cavernous hole in my heart.

The family rarely talked openly about Mom's death; that was how they modeled their way to deal with most problems, by ignoring them. I remember only two times of direct reference to her death from my father. I asked him what caused Mom's heart attack and he answered only, "It was just her time." At the age of 39? That's all?! What kind of an explanation was that? What was my place in this medical mystery?

When I was an older teenager he attempted to discipline me with guilt, "Your mother wouldn't want you to do that..." I hollered back at him, "You don't know what she would want. She's dead!" This was one of the few times that I consciously let out any clue of my anger and despair; I was way too afraid of touching that pain.

I didn't properly process my mother's death until decades later; it seems like eons that I held onto feelings of abandonment, self-pity, confusion, anger, depression. Of course such feelings are natural reactions to trauma, but I sure could have used help dealing with these powerful emotions. My pain just kept growing inside of me while I showed my "good-girl" veneer to others and they marveled at my strength. In hindsight, I did have inner strength but my way would have been much easier had my emotional needs been recognized.

A New Healing Path Begins

The hindsight in this healing process is fascinating! Reviewing my healing journey so far, I have complete trust that the present moment is perfect and every day my life weaves another piece of the pattern. My very intimate relationship with Spirit has always held me upright in tough times, even though it took a while to consciously recognize the amazing power of that connection. Small wonder that I was drawn to teaching and energy healing as a career.

Following my ever-present urge to teach and guide, I received my BS degree in Education, taught for a while, and finished graduate work in social psychology. In the 1960's and 70's creativity was encouraged and I took it upon myself to pay extra attention to the less-fortunate kids who needed healthy doses of self-esteem. No doubt it was love and respect that helped them grow, far more than any curriculum.

My personal pattern of following the urge to broaden my horizons led me to willingly step away from teaching, get married at 25, move to Texas, then Colorado, and then California where I gave birth to my beautiful daughter, Danica, when I was 32. I sorely missed my mother's presence at my marriage and during my baby's growth, but I could often feel Dorothy's love warmly touching my heart. Her unique recognizable presence would always ease my loneliness a bit.

The ability to feel vibrations and sense my mother's presence led me to deeply and broadly explore the spiritual world. The more I learned, the more I developed a thirst for spiritual wisdom and slowly began to awaken to the understanding that, though undisciplined, I have been an intuitive healer all my life.

I trained in several different healing modalities and was blessed with some beautiful teachers. But instead of staying with any one way of looking at energy work, I added new skills and techniques to my increasing intuitive abilities to connect with

Spirit. I love all kinds of healing work, from individual clients to groups, to teaching, to channeling and writing; but at some point always find myself getting antsy, wanting to expand my spiritual experiences.

So it was one day that I discovered an exciting healing path when an employment announcement popped up on LinkedIn. I rarely looked at those lists, never expecting to see companies seeking energy healers. But there it was: Hospice of the Chesapeake in Maryland was looking for Reiki volunteers. I had often thought about using my healing gifts in hospitals and with troubled youngsters, but never had I considered the needs of terminally ill patients. It simply wasn't a thought. Yet I didn't think twice before calling Hospice; I had no doubts that this was the new work I wanted!

I became completely absorbed in the training and within a couple of weeks, I was visiting my first hospice patient. It didn't take long to fall in love with this special work. For the first time in my life, I was able to accept death as a part of life; this was the beginning of healing my own grief for sure. It was such an honor to help people gently feel their spiritual connection before transitioning out of this life.

Alison, the volunteer coordinator, was one of many angels who helped shift my life. She was totally supportive of the Reiki work but she had never experienced energy healing herself, so we arranged a meeting time at the office. That day Alison came in frazzled; it had been chaotic at work as usual and she could barely think straight, but she agreed to a short energy session anyway. It was less than 5 minutes after the energy began to flow through my hands to her energy field that Alison contentedly sighed and visibly relaxed on the office couch. Shortly after this time, she and I planned the first offering of my Loving Shift training to staff and volunteers, leading participants to feel the movement of healing energy for themselves.

I continued patient visits and classes for over two years until I again felt the urge for change and moved to western Colorado, where I had visited my daughter for quite a few years. No surprise that after settling in, the first place I contacted was Hope West, the hospice organization serving western Colorado. My work started out with patients and classes, and I then established *Loving Shift* as my personal energy healing practice. After just a few months, I met another angel named Mel and began a new personal healing chapter.

Mel, the new Hope West Bereavement Coordinator, asked if I would join her group of volunteers. I was as quick to commit to the bereavement group as I had been to join Hospice in the beginning! Once again, new things were moving in to joyously fill my life.

Not only did Mel and I become special friends, but we helped each other immensely in our growth. I introduced her to energy healing and she introduced me to the ins-and-outs of healthy bereavement. I also helped some of Mel's bereavement clients release their emotions energetically.

The bereavement work is for me as beautifully profound as the energy healing with terminal patients. There are so many incredible ways to shift our lives when we're ready to do so! It warms my heart to remember the time when I was able to lead a widow out of her panic attack by guiding her to move out her own anxious energy. She later reported that she felt the shift happen and that her panic attacks never returned.

Heal Thyself

The next step for me was to take formal bereavement training so that I could be included in hospice group sessions. For the first set of group gatherings, I was there as a shadow, to learn by being a member of the group.

Mel asked us each to tell why we were there and name the person we were grieving. I hadn't been expecting such a question, and I said something akin to *I have had many losses but I suppose if I were to name the one loss that grieves me most, that would be my mother, Dorothy.*

Well, duh...

As I opened up to my own grief, I realized how much my life had been impacted by my mother's death. Over the years, the sadness would swallow me up with depression at unexpected times. The fact that my mother wasn't around to protect me led to a pattern of looking to other people to show me the way, but I usually end up feeling overly dependent and disappointed. I tended to avoid conflict like the plague because I couldn't let the suppressed pain and anger bubble up and eat me alive.

Talking about my mother was a great catharsis. Mel was a beautiful guide, constantly encouraging in a safe way. When I continued with more spiritual energy healing on my own, I was so grateful to have had such a compassionate mentor. Learning that grieving has a strong spiritual aspect was at first hard for me to grasp, but upon releasing sadness, I allowed that closed part of my heart to awaken. My spirit always came rushing in to help, especially the day I met Dorothy in the mountains.

Talking with Dorothy

My daughter and I were camping for the second time in the Uncompaghre Forest in Western Colorado. We had planned to spend at least three days, but on the second morning, I woke up feeling out of sorts; my chest was a little tight and my breathing was shallow. The October weather was beginning to take a turn toward cold and rainy anyway, so we decided to go back home.

Once we were all packed up, Danica left to take the dog for one last hike. I didn't go because I knew that I'd slow them down, so I waited in the warm car. Perusing a book on bereavement by Alan Wolfelt, I found myself musing once again on my own pain around Mommy's death. I felt the sadness physically as my shoulders drooped a little and my chest felt even heavier than when I had first woken up. But if you had looked in the car window at that moment, you would have figured I was idly daydreaming with a book open on my lap.

There I was, thinking about my mother, when the energy surrounding me instantly shifted. I took a couple of deep breaths and my chest felt lighter than air, like I was in my own personal bubble. I just knew that I was connecting with Mom because it was the kind of knowing that resonated deeply from my soul and expanded with the calmness of pure love. I was aware of Dorothy's energetic presence with every cell in my being as we spoke without words but with perfect understanding. That kind of communication can be next to impossible to explain but once you know that energy, you know it.

As we communicated soul to soul, I clearly grasped that there was no hierarchy or delineation of mother and daughter. We are, always have been, and always will be soul sisters!!

We came together to share some things in this lifetime. We are totally equal and share an unbreakable bond of love. I inhaled the limitless in our connection of love and forever erased any belief of abandonment or loss.

Dorothy slowly faded from focus and I began to slide into the awareness of my body in the car in the mountains, feeling peaceful and whole in every part of my being. That magnificent feeling remains to this day every time I think of my mother and I relish connecting with her energy. What an awesome healing shift!

The heart of hospice knows no bounds.

Hospice

Volunteering for Hospice has been one of the true joys of my life. Years ago, I had been thinking that I was ready for something more expansive in my energy healing work when "out of the blue" an ad showed up on my computer on LinkedIn, wanting Reiki practitioners to work with patients. I didn't think twice about the idea; within five minutes I was on the phone to Hospice of the Chesapeake in Maryland and started training the next week.

This beautiful work was expansive indeed! I deeply appreciated the beauty in helping a person be at ease in their situation and to pass on peacefully. May we all be that blessed. Working with bereaving families and teaching others how to feel energy is grand, but it's a most unique joy to see someone fill with love as they become ready to transition Home.

I kept notes of my impressions so that I could remember these wonderful people I met in hospice. For purposes of sharing, I give fictitious names for each person but there is nothing made up about the experiences!

Betty

The first time I visited 60-year-old Betty, she was slumped in her wheelchair and seemed slightly nervous; she had suffered a stroke and had had several anxiety attacks. It was projected that she had only a few months to live. Betty wasn't sure of why I was there so she opted to stay sitting in her wheelchair when I explained that I would help her to balance her energy. After two or three minutes of my hands on her shoulders, Betty nodded drowsily and asked her nurse to help her onto the bed.

She immediately closed her eyes and deeply relaxed during the next half hour of concentrated energy flow. Betty suddenly startled, opened her eyes, and exclaimed, "I saw Mama! I saw my Mama!"

She was too excited to lie down again so the nurse helped her back into her wheelchair. We talked for a bit about what she saw and felt during the energy flow. She quietly told me, "This was quite a journey."

After a short while she became a bit anxious and wiggled restlessly in her chair. Betty complained to me, "I know I should calm down. Why can't I calm down?"

I put my hand on her heart and guided Betty to visualize calming white light moving through her being. After a couple of quiet minutes, she looked up and told me calmly, "I'm not scared anymore."

I had the privilege of being with Betty for the next year and a half. I witnessed her crying; I witnessed her moods change;

I witnessed her pain both lessen and increase. I did not witness another anxiety attack. During one healing session when I was moving energy around her head, she smilingly said that she was remembering her father and how his touch would always calm her down.

It was my joy to share this precious time with Betty. She changed my life as much as I did hers. But then, that's what happens when Love is shared.

Elizabeth

I visited Elizabeth only one time before she passed. She was in a large nursing facility and I had no idea what to expect. I asked at the nurses' station if there was any particular time that was best to visit and she said kindly, "It doesn't matter when you come. She is how she is. Just pop in and out."

I understood what the nurse was talking about because Elizabeth was completely unresponsive with her eyes closed. After being there only a couple of minutes, the housekeeping person asked me to step out for 5 minutes so that she could mop the floor. When I returned, the housekeeper said, "She opened her eyes when you left. She must recognize your voice." Of course, we had never met before but she recognized something alright!

I first sat on the chair near the foot of her bed and simply sent loving energy to Elizabeth. Then I stood up and went to her side, touched her shoulder and quietly said, "Hi Elizabeth, I'm Ronna. I'm here from Hospice. I just want you to know that I am here. That's all. I'm here."

I kept my hand lightly on her shoulder and she opened her eyes wide. She looked at me and moved slightly, though I couldn't guarantee that she actually recognized my physical presence. I spoke her name again and then sat back down in the chair. She looked around a few more times and then closed her eyes again.

Never again will I underestimate how much our loving presence can indeed be felt!

Marsha

Marsha took my Loving Shift class at Hospice of the Chesapeake; she was not a hospice volunteer but wanted to learn more about energy healing for her own development. She loved the class and told me a couple of weeks later that she wanted to continue with this learning.

Of course I was happy to hear this news and gladly agreed to be her mentor. She called a couple of weeks later, "Ronna! I must tell you about the amazing phone call I had!" Who wouldn't be interested in hearing?!

Marsha had spent the last week at the beach with her friend, Anna. Near the end of the vacation, Anna was feeling pretty depressed. Her fiancé had died only the year before and her grief was still very strong.

Marsha explained how she began to soothe Anna; she stroked her hair and spoke lovingly to her. She then used the breathing she learned in class and let the energy pour from her heart through her fingertips. She intuitively began to sweep away the negative energy and understood that she needed to gently tell Anna that it was time to let go of her grief.

Marsha returned home the next day and received a call from Anna two days later. Anna told Marsha that she had no idea what had occurred on Sunday, but her deep grief and pain were now gone.

Eddie

I knocked when I first got to Eddie's house and there was no answer. I rang the doorbell and there was still no answer. Checking my papers to see that I had the right address and the right time, I opened the door and poked my head in. Heading slowly toward the door was a man in his seventies, sporting a cane and partially paralyzed by palsy. He invited me in by curling and waving his fingers, much like a young child's greeting.

I introduced myself and explained that I was there to do some Reiki with him. He maneuvered himself onto his bed and lowered the head down so that he was lying flat; he obviously understood what we were going to do. Eddie tried to speak a few times during our session and I had to put my ear next to his mouth to understand. I did get "this is wonderful" and "you are a good woman." I could see that at one time Eddie must have been quite the charmer! I caught sight of his partner as I was leaving; Kent introduced himself and told me that he was not at all convinced about the validity of energy work but he was honoring Eddie's wishes.

Eddie seemed more spry the next week and he was actually using his voice somewhat. He relaxed into the energy work and I could see his whole body let go. His partner came in afterwards and told me how much Eddie likes the energy work and spoke very highly of hospice and its services. Eddie nodded his head and smiled in agreement.

Then Kent showed me around the house, pointed out Eddie's art designs and the three of us went out to the garden area that Eddie had earlier designed. I felt completely welcomed and comfortable in their place.

A couple of weeks later, Kent met me at the door and told me that he was concerned about Eddie. He felt that the prescribed medication was too strong and could be causing Eddie to feel depressed, as he had been down and relatively unresponsive for at least three days. We went out to the back deck, warmed by the new spring sunshine, and I balanced energy with Eddie for at least an hour. At one point, Eddie muttered that he could hear the birds singing and feel the breezes. When I finished the session and asked how he felt, Eddie looked right at me bright eyes and a big grin and said, "I feel as light as a feather."

Later that day, I received this email from Kent: "Ronna, ever since you left here, Eddie has felt so much better. You brought him out of three days of depression. You're wonderful." I reiterated to Kent that I, Ronna, did nothing by myself; I act as a conduit for focusing the universal energy. They later went on vacation to the beach and when I arrived at the house the following week, I was amazed at how well Eddie looked. He had trimmed down and toned up and his eyes were flashing with fun. His grin was as charming as could be and his articulation was the clearest I had heard. That special visit made my heart sing and dance for days!

A few weeks later I received this text from Kent:

"Ronna, I love u. Eddie passed gently last nite. Just u know u were exceptional." My heart sang to Eddie.

I have continued for years to give thanks for the wonderful opportunity of meeting Eddie, Kent, Betty, and others and becoming part of their life, as they became part of mine. As I have said throughout *How to Get to Wonderful*, Love has only one need and that need is to be shared.

There is written deeply within each of you a wondrous myth that is your own.

Write Your Personal Myth

Says Bartholomew in the book *I Come as a Gentle Brother*, "There is written deeply within each of you a wondrous myth that is your own. This is the story of your struggle toward consciousness. It is filled with your own personal journey, encompassing both the successes and failures, the tears and the laughter, the expansions and the contractions of your life...If you allow yourself to write your own myth, you can experience directly the strength and wisdom of your own teaching."

I wrote *The Master* stories over a period of two or three years, starting out as the above fascinating exercise to write my personal myth, letting my subconscious lead the way. The stories kept coming to me and after a time, it was clear that the Master, though placed in ancient times, was unfolding my current personal journey of trials and never-changing need to speak of Spirit. The Master is a seeker, a teacher and he's full of questions about life. You will see the story of how he meets up with Amanda, his wise loving soul, or higher self, and together they join with people spreading love from village to village.

Amanda and the Master

Today started out as an ordinary day for me as I was taking my morning stroll in the crisp air of the early hour. And there she was! Relaxing on a flat, gray boulder with her head tilted back towards the morning sun as her auburn locks flowed gracefully toward the ground. Her flowing white gown was dancing around her outstretched legs, beckoning the breezes to come and play.

Her eyes were closed and her face had the look of someone who had just discovered the most luscious secret in the world. The glow that surrounded her expanded in all directions, seemingly without end. The vision of this awe-inspiring being was surreal; yet, at the same time, it felt completely natural and welcoming. I quickly stepped forward to make her acquaintance.

Master: *Amanda! How nice to see you. I didn't expect to find you here this morning. What a delight!*

(Why was I saying this?! I had never met this woman. Why did I greet her like an old friend? How was I so sure she was called Amanda?)

Amanda: Good morning, Master. I trust that you've been enjoying your walk. It is a beautiful day, isn't it?

M: *It most certainly is, indeed. But you know I love this path in all seasons.* (What was I doing?! I was talking with her as if we had known each other for years and that she shared in my morning routine. And why did I feel so relaxed?)

Have you been waiting long?

(Waiting long?! What was I thinking? My poor analytical brain was hitting overload! How could she have been waiting for me if we had never even met? I had just been out on my solitary stroll and I wasn't on the way to meet anyone, let alone someone I had only briefly heard about. And why did I feel so relaxed here?)

A: Oh, Master, I wasn't waiting for you. I've been here all along. I knew you'd see me eventually. And what a wonderful day for your arrival.

M: *I didn't arrive, Amanda. I'm just here.* (Now why did I say that?! What did it mean, anyway?)

Her hearty laugh filled the meadow. The glow surrounding us seemed to quiver and vibrate as I joined in with the fun.

A: I'm glad you are here now. We need each other, you know.

M: *Need each other?*

A: Sure.

M: *Well, it might seem obvious to you, but not to me. You're so, so everything.*

A: That's true. I don't need anything because I am whole all by myself. I'm content. I'm peaceful. I know that I can create whatever I want whenever I want it. I am complete love and I know it. It just doesn't get any better than that. That's why people aspire to be like me. They don't want to be me; they want to feel the same way for themselves. They recognize universal love and they're drawn to it.

M: *But, Amanda, that makes you the true master. Your peacefulness, your wisdom and your grace are what we all desire within ourselves. We're all seekers, hoping to attain that knowledge.*

A: My friend, I am not a master. A master is a teacher. A master takes the knowledge that she gains and offers it to her students. The goal of a great master is to lead the students into ways of attaining their own knowledge.

M: *That sounds like me.*

A: Of course that's you. At least it's a part of you. And that's why we need each other.

M: *I still don't get it. You're whole. You're complete. You're joy. You know just who you are. Why would you possibly need me? Though I have myself felt the bliss and I know theoretically that I truly am the same as you, I don't act that way all the time; I can be plagued by doubts and insecurities.*

And I have these drives: I want to record my inspirations. I want to write them down and have them make wonderful sense. I want to share them! I want to show people how joyous the universe is and I want them to feel the same kind of joy that I do!

A: Why?

M: *Why? Because I love the people and I know what wonders are awaiting us as long as we open our hearts.*

A: Master, you have seen grace in your life. You can feel it when grace expands your life. But you also know that it's your life only that you are charged with enlightening.

M: *I know that.*

A: Then why are you so passionate about others seeking enlightenment?

M: *Because I'm a part of everyone else. What I do affects everyone else and what they do affects me. We're all in this together.*

A: So are you just being selfish? If other people are full of grace, then your life would be easier?

We both laughed a wonderful, hearty giggle that sent the meadow quivering again.

M: *You're right in a way, Amanda. Life would be easier if we were all as full of grace as you and still have the fun and challenge of our adventures.*

A: Okay, Master, here it is. We are two aspects of the same whole and we need to work together. We love people; we love life and we want people to be aware of their own power. Each person's gain is everybody's gain because we are all connected.

M: *Right.*

A: I am complete in that my love and my divine connection simply are; I know that and I live it. People are drawn to the love because they know within themselves that they are love too. They want to drink it in. They want love's comfort as well as love's power.

M: *Absolutely.*

A: But, because I am whole and completely at peace, I have no needs. I simply am. I'm a symbol of the grace to which people aspire when they see that they, too, can become love-filled. Simply by my manner, I offer encouragement.

M: *That's most important.*

A: Yes, encouragement is important. It's necessary for beings to see for themselves what they can achieve in potential. However, support alone is not enough.

M: *Not enough?*

A: No. Not enough for most. Once someone understands *what* is possible in a life run by love energy, then they need to learn *how* to achieve that feeling. And that's where you come in.

M: *I see.*

A: Your drives are no accident. They are your gifts. Your ambitions to teach and talk to people and to write about spiritual things are the manner in which you serve. You teach people in ways that they can understand. You teach them how to recognize potential and how to access it for themselves. You invite them to *come along* and you show them how. Just as you have spent this lifetime learning from your myriad of teachers, so are you now a teacher to others. It's a very wonderful position to be a master.

M: *I do love it.*

A: Of course. And, it's constantly stimulating and exciting. It satisfies your personality, does it not?

M: *It does. And the filled quiet satisfies you?*

A: It does indeed.

Grins, nudges and the silence of delight.

A: What a team . . .

M: **That's why I felt that I knew you already! I do know you. We're parts of the same whole!**

A: You bet. And though we are parts of the same One, we represent different aspects: grace and logic, heart and mind, working as one.

M: *As humans we aspire to grace. We seek a life that is full and fulfilling and peaceful. We know that we have conflicts but we desire to learn from our hard times and find solutions out of love.*

A: Yet as one of grace, I have no drive to teach. I simply am... whole and complete.

M: *True. And I, as a human, am here to learn about myself and to heal any parts of me that keep love at a distance. I'm naturally endowed with needs and drives because they keep me on the path of healing, shifting to wholeness.*

A: Precisely. And together with spirit, heart, and mind working as one, we can help others to understand and know how truly wonderful they are.

A&M: *Now is the time to begin! Let's go and light the way!!*

The meadow remained bathed in sunlight and the glow began to spread.

Let compassion and wisdom engulf you and all others who wish to be free.

My Path Continues

I experienced this story during a deep relaxed state in which I asked to visit with my Higher Self. This myth is yet another example of connecting to Spirit. I have described the scenes as if I were watching a movie; but I felt the energy of the conversations deeply within my own being.

I was meandering along my favorite forest path smelling the invigorating wintergreen of the yellow birch, when I heard the voices of my Loved Ones, the Light Beings:

LB: Ronna! Come and play! Dance with us!

Ronna: *Where are you? I'm on a winding forest path right now and my vision is narrowed because of the hundreds of trees. I hear you calling but I can't see you.*

LB: Look up, over here where the light shines through the leaves of the birch trees. This forest has kept you from seeing our presence in the meadow.

R: *I can feel you!! The energy you're setting forth has me tingling all over! Oh, how I want to be with you.*

LB: Well then, just step into the opening to your right and join us. We're singing and dancing and flying!!!

R: *Loved Ones, your call is inviting but I don't know if I should step off this familiar path.*

I'm afraid I'll get lost. What if I can't find my way home?

LB: Silly. We are part of your path; just follow the light. You'll see. You're perfectly safe, so come and play!

I cautiously put my right foot forward and then take my left foot off the ground when I instantly find myself standing in the center of a wide circle of twinkling lights.

R: *Wow! I just thought about joining you and here I am!!*

I feel like a whirling dervish, spinning...spinning...spinning... actually dizzy with delight!

Look! Now I'm soaring as a delicate fairy with shiny silver wings. Higher and higher I go...dancing...twirling...gliding to my heart's content!

What joy to all be dancing together here in this light place. How could I possibly have been afraid to be so carefree?!

LB: You don't need to be afraid anymore, now that you know. You're Home. Back on earth we're actually playing a game. Some adventures are scary, some are delightful and some are just plain hard; but they're all games we make up together. We always meet back here to rejoice as our light selves.

R: *I see some familiar energies here:*

Hey Jerry! So nice to see you my dear friend. I wish we had had more time together on earth.

Oh Mattie, I would know you anywhere. Yes, I see you projecting yourself as a proud young woman this time. You are still the same gorgeous beacon of love that I knew when you were a much older woman, always there when I needed you.

Hey Danica, you're grinning and dancing with us as well! We'll have to do more of this together when we are back in bodies!

I don't know all of the other earthly names right now but it really doesn't matter. I am so content to be totally surrounded by all of you loving light beings. It's magnificently clear that I am one of you and that we are Home!

And here's Mama! My heart quickens as you, the loving light of my soul, reassure me that I most certainly am Home.

Interestingly, *Mama* is showing me two different energetic aspects of herself. First she appears like Aunt Jemima, motherly and nurturing. She is full-of-body and bursting with life! She is the consummate story-teller. This marvelous aspect of my soul is indeed the cosmic mama, oozing wisdom and love.

And here is another related aspect of the cosmic mother. This young *Mama* is a heavenly divine goddess, also bursting with life! Divine energy pours from her being and lights up everyone in her presence.

Says *Mama*:

You know me as facets of yourself that you manifest on earth. I am the cosmic mama, the high Goddess, the divine feminine energy. I am indeed you and a divine aspect of everyone's soul as well.

We are now in a higher and lighter dimension than that which you experience on earth. We call it "The Joyful Place." I am here to remind you that you have work to continue when you leave The Joyful Place. When you return to your physical body on the earth dimension, you must always remember that you are one with the divine aspects of your soul. Always strive to be a joyous, loving energy. Do whatever will keep you consciously in the light.

Know that you are never alone.

If you feel lost or need help remembering who you truly are, simply say *Remind Me*.

You will let others know that they, too, can bring this divine joyous energy to earth. Help them to experience the bliss. Show them how to remember love!

The more you play in your human times, the faster you will bring in joy. Remember that this earth life is a game you all play together and your goal is to remember who you really are. Play, create, paint, sing, dance, hug, cry, love...do anything that opens you to your light.

Your consciousness is now returning to the earth dimension. Remain aware that we are with you always. We are here to help.

Open to your light and share your visions with others.

Awaken

Awaken my loves, the dream is over.

In your sleep on earth
you have had adventures and done things,
been things,
thought things,
and felt things.

You were nourished and protected
so that you could grow in your dream play.

Now, Beloveds, you are ready to awaken from the dream.

When you open your eyes, the eyes that lie within your heart, you will see what was hidden in your game of sleep.

With your heart, you will see a universe of indescribable, profound Love.

Feel the Love.
You are this Love.

Feel the flow of your immense, unending joy.
Feel the flow of your immense, unending freedom.

Hear the music you had forgotten.
    Flow with this music,
        This music that sings with your heart.

You are this indescribable music beyond the dream.

    Awaken Beloveds, the dream is over.

The Real is now before you. The True is now before you.
Remember the Truth.
    Remember the Love that you are, that you have been,
    that you always will be.
    No beginning, no end.

Love awaits you
as you awaken from the dream, my loves.

Step by step, moment by moment, come out of the dream.

Feel yourself expand out of the dream state into indescribable, never-ending Love.

Feel your connections to all.

Feel the vibrations and pulsations that reach forever.

Awakened from the dream, you will continue to have earthly adventures as before, but they are now all entwined with Love.

> GREATER,
>
> > GRANDER,
> >
> > > EASIER

than you ever could have dreamt.

Awaken my loves.
Welcome to *Love*.

Take my hand and together we will soar.

Reaching the Heights

To offer a bit of background, the summer of 2020 gave us COVID-19, along with extreme heat and wildfires throughout western Colorado. Red-orange smoke-filled skies, ashes falling in the yard. Burning eyes. Coughing. Nowhere to get away.

Summer 2021 brought extreme heat and drought to Colorado again, especially on the Western Slope. July began the monsoon season there, creating mudslides throughout the barren burn areas in the mountains. Major East-West Highway (I-70) closed to all traffic where water and mud are coming up to or over the road.

It was in this atmosphere that my amazing adventure happened when I needed to get to the Front Range from the high desert of the Western Slope. Having a phobia about heights is not an easy way to be when you live and travel in Western Colorado, unless you never want to go anywhere. Reaching the Heights is about how it feels to experience a healing shift when you least expect it.

My fear of heights has caused me a lot of anxiety throughout my life, but as I began applying the Loving Shift methods I had developed over the years, I felt safe enough to experience true healing, step by step. The awesome thing is that when the major shift happens, it's so subtle and so effortless, I almost miss it. So in this story, here I am, scared to death of curvy mountain heights, and needing to get to Denver to catch a flight.

The Adventure Begins

Ugh! I over-packed again...but I can't take any chances of being unprepared in case of...of...well...anything! Okay, let's see... Everything is in the car. Sandwiches and water are next to me and I have plenty of toilet paper, juice, coffee, an extra sweater, a blanket, flashlight, and, of course, plenty of chocolate. Checked on the computer and there was nothing about Glenwood Canyon being closed. Ready for the six-hour trek.

What??! Now the GPS says to take an alternate route because of possible road closures in Glenwood Canyon on I-70 due to mudslides. I could go South and take US 50 East. No, wait...50 is closed on weekdays for summertime construction. Wow. Not so easy to get out of the Valley today.

Let me try a different app. Nope! Looks like they all got the memo: Take an alternate route and add 2-3 hours to your drive. Not a lot of choice here; I'll start out my usual way and then let the GPS lead me home.

What the hell?! I can only go through Aspen? OMG, that sign says Independence Pass is open.

Independence Pass??!! Drop-off edges made me pee in my pants when I was a kid. Oh no, there must be another way to get around Aspen. There has to be!

Okay, okay, let me think... There's a gas station. I'll go in and ask directions.

Seriously?! This road leads to Independence Pass and there's no alternative route?! I've always been terrified of the Pass! On such a steep and narrow road, I am likely to try and slide under the glove box and still have a death grip on the door handle.

I don't dare glance out because if the road sees me looking, I swear it will magnetically pull the car over the edge.

Sure, you say it's safe if I just go slow, but what about the narrow road and the steep edges?! Oh lordy...

Okay, deep breath... It's not feasible to turn around. There's nowhere to go anyway. The other route is all the way back past where I started and then it would take 8 hours from there! And who knows what mountains those roads go over?!

I've got this... Roads don't really magnetize cars, I'm safe. I won't think about where I'm headed and just focus on driving the car. That's all I need to do. I'm just part of this long line of cars slowly going through Aspen.

Almost through town. Signs say no large vehicles allowed. Must mean that I'm headed to Independence Pass now... Breathe... Breathe...

See? This isn't so bad...nice and slow with nothing to throw me off balance. Oh, that's why we're creeping along. We're stuck behind a big fat RV, going less than 20 mph. That's okay though; slow feels safe. Oops, RV is too wide, waiting for on-coming traffic to give it some room. Wow. No wonder they post size limits.

Finally...the RV got past the narrow part of the road and we're going a little faster. No problem, I've got this.

God it's beautiful up here. Haven't felt this special high altitude air for years; I had forgotten such peacefulness. It's magnificent. I love you mountains!

Maybe a quick glance to the side?

Whoa, here's the deep valley I remember that just keeps dropping, and those high rocky slopes across the valley.

Ooooh, my stomach didn't drop. My knuckles aren't white. My chest isn't tight and I'm breathing almost like normal.

Wow. Look at that beautiful alpine meadow and the red and yellow flowers on that bush....

Wait a minute...I'm looking around and enjoying the view!

I've already crossed the heights!

Holy crap! I did it!

I moved a mountain today.

The following are words from a Master and Amanda myth 15 years before this amazing adventure took place:

"You always have enjoyed being somewhere but you don't particularly like the getting there part. In fact, it often makes you anxious and you worry about all the many things that could happen along the way. Yet the trip to somewhere is usually one of the most wonderful parts, and you see and experience many things that you would miss if you were simply transported from one place to the next. Your memories hold the trip there as fondly as the destination, sometimes more so."

Indeed.

The Mark of Love

It's time to set aside your troubles for the moment and let love come in and fill you up.

As you put down your burdens and tie them in an old bag, feel your heaviness begin to release.
Feel the space around you become lighter.
Feel this space around you fill with the lightness of love.

Let this love come in through the top of your head and infiltrate every part of your being.

Feel the light glow inside your head.
Feel the glow on your face, smooth and soft.
Feel the lightness glide down your neck and your shoulders. Your muscles let go. There is nothing they need to hold on to.

Let the lightness of love continue down your arms and out your fingertips to join the world.

Bring the lightness down your spine, branching out to the muscles in your back and around to your heart, your breast and your chest. Be light down to your hips and pelvis, adding to the very strength that supports you.

Let this love and light continue down your legs and to your feet that keep you so well rooted into this earth.

Let the love slip through the bottom of your feet into the earth.

Know that the peacefulness of love reaches down deep into the earth ...above into infinity ...and everywhere within you.

Bundled in your blanket of love, see yourself begin to rise. Float above the tops of the houses,
above the trees,
past the birds,
to the clouds.

Sit upon any cloud you like.
Feel its gentle cushion of support.

Let yourself simply be.

With your higher awareness, look down upon the earth. So that you can better understand the burden you have left behind, allow yourself to be aware of the places and people and areas that are filled with fear and hate. See these fearful pockets now.

Feel the effect of this hate reflected in your own physical body. Where you just felt expansive with love, now sense the constriction of fear. Feel the fear in your muscles. Feel the fear in your gut. Feel the tightness in your heart.

Feel how much of this fear has been accepted on our dear earth. You can sense it.
Sense its color.
Sense its shape.

Come in for a closer view and see the fear in individuals. Sense their energy and understand them, because you know fear's effects.

Feel the sadness.
Feel the heaviness.
Feel how hard it is to move in the thickness of hate.

See the individuals plodding along, trying to move in the sludge of fear. See them clump together, fear clinging to the groups.

Feel the sorrow that fear creates
so that you can better understand.

Now that you understand, shake off the heaviness.
Move your shoulders and shake your head.
Throw off the fearful energy. Let it vaporize and disappear.

Breathe deeply.
Come back to your loving self.

Look down again at the world,
but look with different eyes.

See a wispy blanket of love spread over the earth.
You can see the love.
Sense its color.
Sense its form.

Feel Love's lightness, the lightness that is also you.

Let Light permeate the entire earth and the beings on this earth. See the darkness dissipate.

See fear transform to love and watch darkness turn to light.

As the world becomes lighter and freer with love, look down and see that there are no longer separate, heavy individuals. There are no isolated heavy groups.

See that people are all brilliant specters of light.

Notice the light from every individual reach out and blend with the light of everyone else.

See the joy as people join together to love and laugh and dance and hug. Watch as Love weaves in and around every being and joins with all the others.

Feel the joy and see how the world has been transformed by the fires of love.

See our world as a world of light spreading greater ...and greater ...and greater.

Sense the Love and Light that has reached you and now flows through every cell of your being.

This same Love is reaching out right now to every other being on earth.

See the transformation on earth.
See that with Love there is no separation.

Understand the struggle. See those who are waiting for light.

Send the Light of Love to every yet dark spot in our world and every being to transform them.

As an individual can make a mark in the world through hate, so does an individual make an even greater mark through Love.

Know that in an instant you can replace heaviness with the lightness of Love.

Send Love wherever it is needed.
Send Love to the leaders of our world's countries.
Send Love to those who have the power to make decisions for others.
Send Love to those who feel they have no power.

Let others feel the great transforming power of Love.

Slowly begin to return your awareness to your physical body.

Let Love continue to move lightly through you and from you.

Watch Love spread as it connects light to light in a world of love that we continue to create.

Make your mark on the world.

First written in remembrance of September 11, 2001 when the Twin Towers in New York City came down.

Ronna Helene

Water the seeds of love.

Broken Boy

How can such despair and anger exist simultaneously with my divine lightness of being?

While pondering this apparent duality, my focus shifted to the vision of the five-year-old child we adopted. We didn't know at the time that this young boy was a classic example of extreme attachment disorder, or sociopath. Though the social worker did tell us that he'd gone from foster home to foster home his first five years, she made it sound like that was simply a matter of bad luck. I was so anxious to adopt a young child that I ignored the red flags and naïvely believed that he would be fine.

The behavior he expressed in his early visits was cute and charming, a little guy who would say the right things at the right time. He had perfect manners and a sweet smile. To outsiders, as we prospective parents were at the time, he seemed like a normal kid. We were thrilled to have such a nice little boy with us.

In truth, cute and polite were simply his initial way of gaining people's trust. Love and tenderness were totally unknown emotions to him; even the basic seeds of love lay unplanted.

His mother ignored him in infancy and soon abandoned him, so being attached or bonded to someone was never a concept to be had. Lacking a secure loving identity, the world was a fearful place to him and the motivation for his behaviors was focused outward, based on manipulating and mimicking others in order to feel safe and in control.

Well…having tried earlier for years, I finally became pregnant three months after taking in this child. My obstetrician at the time asked if we were going to keep this boy and I was appalled she could even think such a thing! I committed to his upbringing and we were thrilled that we would have two children now! I loved buying clothes for him, fixing his bedroom, and we even flew our niece out from Oregon to take care of him when I gave birth. He said that he was excited to become a big brother. I didn't understand yet that his words had no truth behind them.

Louise Penny, in her book *Glass Houses*, offers the clearest description of a sociopath that I have seen: "We're used to the film versions of psychopaths. The clearly crazies. But most psychopaths (sociopaths) are clever. They have to be. They know how to mimic human behavior. How to pretend to care, while not actually feeling anything except perhaps rage and an overwhelming and near-perpetual sense of entitlement. That they've been wronged. They get what they want mostly through manipulation. Most don't have to resort to violence…Unlike most of us, who tend to be transparent, people rarely see through a psychopath. He's masterful. People trust and believe him. (They) even like him. It's his great skill. Convincing people that his point of view is legitimate and right, even when all the evidence points in the other direction."

Living with this child after less than a year made me feel crazier every day; my world was upside down and whirling out of control. My moral compass is ingrained with the qualities of love and compassion and I naturally expect some semblance of caring from others. The destructive actions and empty emotions of this young person simply did not make any sense to me; I had no mental space in which to file such behavior. I felt helpless and became increasingly withdrawn; wishing he would just go away somehow. My husband became visibly angrier, and our little daughter was simply confused.

He was with us for almost five years, until he turned 11, and I came to a gradual understanding of just how emotionally empty he is. He refused to make eye contact and showed no emotional responses whatsoever. Admittedly, some of his actions did appear to be somewhat normal, but unacceptable, troubled-childhood behavior, like stealing, ripping out the hems of curtains and painting his bedroom wall with nose buggers. But most frustrating was that any attempt to discipline him or explain why such behavior is unacceptable fell on deaf ears. He would simply stare straight ahead without emotions, anger, remorse, excuses, or defensiveness.

Talking to him was literally like speaking to the wall. His outward behaviors were relatively quiet, because quiet is the best way to be sneaky and draw attention away from one's actions. It was years later that I learned he was in the habit of jumping out from under 3-year-old Danica's bed to scare her in the middle of the night or that he constantly whispered things to her about how awful we were. She was too afraid to tell us. The longer his deceitful presence wore us down, the more our own personal weaknesses came to the forefront, so it probably wasn't a super stretch for her to believe what he said. This young boy, filled with inner rage in an otherwise empty emotional void, had already learned the art of gaslighting.

Such dark and heavy energy is very difficult to ignore, especially disguised as some innocent action, and the emptiness it created was intolerable. I finally called the county mental health office in tears because I could feel myself losing a grasp on reality, like the time I pulled the blanket over my head and refused to leave the couch. (My husband nicknamed me "Turtle" after that.) I felt in a constant state of confusion as I simply could no longer handle the dark energy and I hated the despair and anger that I was experiencing. My sense of self was disintegrating to the point that I couldn't recognize my own self-worth or who I truly was. During therapy, we sadly heard story after similar story of broken marriages and desperate behaviors.

Other than therapy, we had very little emotional support in our trials. We would hear from family and some friends that we were picking on the child, that we just wanted to favor our daughter, that we were stupid, inept, uncaring. My brother said we should send the boy to him, after all he knew "how to treat a child...." I was so tempted to do just that but couldn't bring myself to knowingly destroy my ignorant brother's world.

My mother-in-law had us leave the boy with her for a week and by the time we picked him up, she told us in no uncertain terms that he was never to come back to her house. Later, after only a short weekend with the child, my father just sadly shook his head. They couldn't understand the bizarre things he did and the coldness of his being was an anathema. Nobody knew why, but everyone felt angry and depleted after being around him.

We stubbornly and naively tried for the next 4 years to see love blossom forth, until the day his fourth-grade teacher called us literally screaming that we had to get him out of her classroom! We called Social Services to take him for a respite and he was completely stone-faced when they came to pick him up. He showed no concern whatsoever that he was being moved somewhere else.

The day of his leaving our home, he snuck out of his bedroom and whispered to our four-year-old daughter that we were sending him away. He told her that whenever we say that we love her, that should be the warning to her that we were going to send her away as well. After he left, I found Danica sucking her thumb and staring straight ahead while hiding under a chair. She refused to talk to me. Of course, I had no clue of the ideas he had placed in her head so I encouraged her to come out and kept telling her how much I love her.

It took a long time for each of us to begin to heal from the wounds of this five-year-long, wrenching experience. I had to give up the illusion that with enough love I could fix this child. Though I came to deeply and sadly understand how lack of love creates a miserable existence for everyone involved, I was unable to grasp for years why adopting this person may have been important to my own inner growth. I got the concept of love needing to be shared in order to grow. I felt how scary the world could be without the safety of knowing that you are loved. I witnessed the empty hole that's created by lack of love. Yet I knew there was something more I needed to understand before I could truly heal from this miasma.

While revisiting the what-do-I-need-to-know-about-this-whole-experience question many years later, a vision popped in to teach me. I saw his image and felt the emotional energy of this boy; in my mind's eye I could see clearly how his beautiful point of divine light is trapped within his body. His energy is so dark and dense that the life force energy within him can't flow as it is designed to do.

Broken Boy is in his essence a divine being, as we all are, but because his heart is blocked, loving energy can neither get in nor move out to others. His frozen emotions block the free flow of energy, so love cannot be shared. Hopefully one day he will become aware of his own divine light and finally sense real love.

This vision taught me well: The light of our being is who we truly are. Nothing else is real.

Broken Boy is tied to the following Welcome Birna story because they both speak of the magnificent light of our being. I saw the boy's deeply hidden light and in my Birna vision, I used the light to heal and give others the chance to do the same.

The light of our being is who we truly are.

Welcome Birna

My personal vision of BIRNA is the highlight of my struggles to understand and heal my own deeply seated wounds. BIRNA describes a profound healing session in which I reclaimed my spiritual power and transformed dark energies into the Light of Love.

This true story is the unfolding of my awesome Jin Shin TARA trauma healing session, thanks to the wisdom of practitioner Christine Palafox in western Colorado. I thought I was coming to Christine for some help with my troublesome gut, but this healing was oh so much more.

Christine: *What is your emphasis of concern for this session?*

Ronna: My gut. I know the problems are probably emotionally related, but I've tried everything I can think of and I don't know how to fix them.

C: *Ok, I will be asking you what you feel in different points of your body as I hold points of energy pathways in that place. First, I will lead you into relaxation.*

I initially felt like I wanted to cry but that emotion left almost immediately. As soon as Christine touched my feet, I could feel the energy moving strongly through them. My legs were tingling like crazy and I was compelled to wiggle my toes to help release the energy. Within a few minutes, I was barely able to feel my body on the massage table; I felt light and free and gloriously relaxed. But soon thereafter, I began to fidget a bit.

C: *What are you feeling right now?*
R: My chest is tight and it's hard to breathe.
C: *Stay with this feeling and observe what you experience.*
R: I feel a lot of fear.
C: *Keep watching and find out more about what that fear is ready to reveal to you.*

R: I sense the people who want to silence my spirit and take away my power. Their outright lies and manipulations confuse me and I feel like I must hold on tight to my senses; if I relax my guard, I have no other support and will fall hard. This empty confused feeling they leave me with is painful; it makes my heart ache.

C: *How do they try to silence your spirit?*
R: Mostly they berate me and tell me that I'm a nobody; I'm inferior by nature; I don't know anything. If I do what they want, then they will love me. If I don't do what they say, I will suffer for it. I must listen because they know everything. Their truth is *the* truth.

I can't help but take in their harsh words and heavy energy. In my mind, their messages translate to "It's all my fault," "I shouldn't argue," "I'm not loved." I shrink inside and try to make myself invisible at any sign of confrontation, but then I feel afraid and confused with nothing to say.

I don't talk about this with others because I can't stand the idea of someone telling me *how* I should feel or telling me *what* I am feeling. I can't bear the thought of someone stuffing their truth down my throat. I can't stand being belittled, for fear I will always see myself as little. I hate people telling me it is *all my imagination*, because I fear that I might believe them.

C: *That's a remarkable amount of insight revealed to you from your body. What do you need right now? What would help you to be less afraid?*

R: I really want someone to comfort me. I want to hold someone's hand.

C: *You can bring in anyone you want. Who would you like to comfort you now?*

R: I feel my mother approaching and she is putting her hands on my shoulders.

C: *Does this feel comforting to you now?*

R: No, not really. She loves me but she can't help me.

I understand from her that I need to find my own voice myself.

Mom's familiar energy starts slipping away and I am again alone. Furthermore, my stomach has been rumbling like mad throughout this whole conversation. It's becoming more intense and shoots out gurgles that seem louder than my words. I wonder how Christine can even hear me.

R: I don't feel right... My heart is beating so fast I can hardly breathe!

C: *Can you describe what is happening?*

Led by the Broken Boy, the manipulators in my life march into the space, all of them wearing gray hoodies to hide who they are, but I recognize most of them anyway...the therapist who implanted false memories, the controlling workshop leader with the enormous ego, the zealots who only want me to follow their religion, the many teachers, the self-proclaimed gurus, the supposedly caring family members...oh so many of the people I had wanted to trust.

They are all talking and mumbling at the same time. The buzz of their voices gets louder and louder along with my grumbling gut! They hope I will give in to the confusion they're creating so that it will break my spirit. Then they will pretend to take care of me and set me on the "right path."

C: (after more healing dialogue) *I want you now to listen to young, wise Ronna; listen to her inner wisdom that absolutely knows what is best. What does she want to do?*

I begin to wave my hands in a sweeping dismissive manner, pushing away from my body, pushing them out.

R: Go away!! You can't be here anymore!! You will never have my spirit!

My gut is creating an even greater uproar at this point! I sit up, move my shoulders back, take a deep breath and allow my chest to expand. White light literally beams forth from my heart and covers every person.

I watch in awe as the hoodies begin to fall off the bodies one by one. The hoods disappear down their backs first, followed by the rest of the fabric dropping from the shoulders of each person.

When their cover-ups simply melt into nothingness, each personality is standing there feeling powerless without the pretense of a cloak to hide under. These empty beings now seem very small and vulnerable. I take another deep breath and beam more white light, still in awe as the people and their bodies evaporate all at once.

The space is now filled with points of brilliant white light!
These lights are the true essence of each soul and I speak to the souls with utter confidence and sincerity:
"I see who you really are.
You are only love.
You are free now.
And so am I.

Go and be whatever you want, wherever you want.
The fear you felt no longer exists.
The fear you planted in my head no longer exists.
It is gone from me and from all time.

All gone."

My uproarious gut is now totally silent!!
I take another deep breath, feeling calm, free, and full of life. I can feel that my distress is gone…all gone.

Says Christine, *"I can see why you are such a warrior against illusion and dogma. What word would describe you now as this champion of empowerment?"*
No words come to mind immediately so I lay quietly on the table, letting thoughts drift through my mind as a myriad of images slowly float by. Then the random floating stops and large block letters appear in my consciousness:
BIRNA

The name BIRNA pulses and expands, filling me with its amazing energy. I sense that I am everything all at once. I feel completely grounded and at one with Mother Earth, as I simultaneously connect to other dimensions, to Spirit.

I hear a deep voice speaking my new name into a cavernous space.

BIRNA

BIRNA

BIRNA

booming.....echoing..... reverberating.....

The resounding energy fills the depths of the Black Canyon. Its strong vibrations bounce along the steep canyon walls and expand effortlessly far into the ethers.

I lay quietly on the table, slowly breathing and soaking up this wondrous vision. My mind butts in, questioning what these letters actually mean, and it soon becomes clear when Christine asks me to illustrate my healing session.

I draw the name BIRNA in large block letters, making sure to illustrate the creative fires of red and yellow that I saw in my vision. To further allow this healing shift to become a part of my being, Christine encourages me to dance in order to integrate the new feelings into my physical being. So I simply let my hips lead the way across the room in a slow, thoughtful dance.

After a minute or so, I stretch my arms high above my head, take a deep breath, and bring them down between my knees. Then I bring my hands above my head again, palms up, like holding a precious package, honoring a wonderful new birth!

BIRNA
Birth of Ronna

BIRNA
Connection of Spirit and Earth

This powerful healing shift to love continues to profoundly affect my life. The light always brings me back to my center where I am both grounded and expansive at the same time. Most of the triggers that caused me to feel afraid and alone are simply non-existent now.

I commonly transform heavy thoughts by consciously enveloping myself in white light. When I feel angry or insecure, I do my utmost to get back to remembering that every one of us is a being of divine light, no matter what our personalities may be doing in this game of life. We are here to learn and play and help this earth to hold more love.

In the end, love is all that matters.

Going Home with Mama

Come, my children,
Gather round and feel the warmth of the fire.

Feel how the gentle heat curls around your arms and toes like a blanket.

Let that lovely heat surround you and make you feel warm, inside and out.

Settle into your warm blanket. Let your thoughts all turn into fluffy clouds and see them drift slowly away, like the rising smoke.

See them float into the sky and spread all over.

See how they all drift and blend together.
Your clouds are now joining with everyone else's clouds.

It's beautiful, isn't it?

Now that we are gliding along, let's go on a visit.

Where to?

It's a place called Home.
It's your Home.
It's my Home.
In fact, it's everyone's Home.
And it's all the same place.

How do we get there?

Close your eyes and take my hand.
Take your friend's hand, too, if you would like.
We're going to float along with the clouds.

Just move along with the breeze.
Touch the tops of the trees.
Say hello to the birds.

We're going higher now. Up and up we float.
Keep holding my hand as we fly.

See how light we are?!

I can see Home now.
Can you see it too? Can you feel it?

Oh yes, it makes you tingle all over.
It feels so warm and cuddly,
And so friendly.

It's very bright. There's light everywhere.
Come, let's float into that light.

Oh my, it feels wonderful.
See how you are full of that wonderful light now.

Can you tell who's here?
Can you hear your welcome?

Feel yourself being rocked.
Feel that love.

See all the clouds and lights that have floated together into one big light.

You are part of that light!

Stay here for a while if you like. Feel the love. Be with the light.
Just float......
Just be.....

I know this feels familiar. That's because it's Home.
It's where you came from.
It's where you know who you really are.

You can come back here any time.
Any time you want to.
Because now you know the way.

You can play and have fun here on earth
and you are really never away from Home.

Just close your eyes and let your thoughts drift into clouds.

Simply remember who you are.
You are light and love
and it feels so good.

Float on your clouds now.
Feel the warmth of the fire.
Snuggle into your blanket.

I know your dreams will be sweet.

I love you,

Mama

About the Book

How to Get to Wonderful is a composite of original stories, myths, and prose that demonstrate the awesomeness of connecting with the Universe. Ronna uses the art of storytelling to relate the magnificent healing energy that she has experienced and the visions that brought this energy to life. She has a unique ability to let her readers experience how it actually feels to be love and light in our humanness. Her work is known for its universal appeal—there's something wonderful for everyone.

About the Author

Ronna Helene Webb, MS, has degrees in education and social psychology, is a certified Reiki Master, and a certified End-of-Life Specialist. She also loves being involved in community theater and improv on the western slope of Colorado. Ronna has a gift for clearly translating intuitive energy messages into words that we can understand and feel in our hearts. As she relates her fascinating journey of healing, she touches the divine feminine to guide the listeners to their own strength and inner power.

www.ingramcontent.com/pod-product-compliance
Lightning Source LLC
Chambersburg PA
CBHW071135090426
42736CB00012B/2126